# Watch Out for the Pointy End:

## Knife Defence Manual to Assist in Training Citizens, Law Enforcement and Security Personnel

Rick Wilson

Photographs by Chris Beaton

Edited by BD Wilson

# WARNING

Some of the techniques and drills contained in this book are extremely dangerous and could cause injury or death. It is not the intent of the author, publisher or distributors of the book to encourage readers to attempt any of these techniques or drills without proper professional supervision and training. Attempting to do so can result in severe injury or death. Do not attempt any of these techniques or drills without the supervision of a certified instructor.

The author, publisher and distributors of this book do not make any representation or warranty regarding the legality or appropriateness of any technique contained in this book.

Specific self defence responses illustrated in this book may not be justified in any particular situation in view of the totality of circumstances or under the law for the applicable jurisdiction.

The author, publisher and distributors of this book do not make any representation or warranty regarding the effective application of any technique contained in this book due to the totality of circumstances that pertain to any self defence response.

The author, publisher and distributors of this book disclaim any liability from damage or injuries of any type that a reader or user of information contained in this book may encounter from the use of said information.

Consult a physician before engaging in the techniques and drills contained in this book and only under supervision of a certified instructor.

This book is presented for academic study only.

## Dedication

This is dedicated to my wonderful wife, Andrea, without whom I would be nothing and have nothing.

# Contents

# Foreword

I've been waiting for this book for awhile. Well, maybe not this book. I've been waiting for Rick to get off his ass and write pretty much any book.

For every famous martial artist you've heard of, there are at least ten who are better that you've never heard of. These are the men and women who devote a lifetime of study to something they love. Some never teach. Some teach to a small group in their garage or basement. Or work out with friends in the park.

Rick Wilson is one of those guys.

His body mechanics are superb. He can explain the principles that underlie the technique you can't quite figure out. And if you want a karate blackbelt from Rick, you will at some point get tossed into a storage container with two armored opponents.

Rick's had a martial arts journey. He studied Uechi-ryu, a traditional Okinawan karate style. And he rejected it. Too old, not in line with modern knowledge, ridiculous. So he went off on his own, as deep into body mechanics as he could. Digging down to understand. And he came full circle. Back to Uechi. Back to tradition.

Remember, systems became traditions by not losing. By not getting wiped out. Somewhere at the root of every old system is a reason why it hasn't disappeared. Too often the core is misunderstood or deliberately obscured. Or obscured because the instructor can hide his ignorance and misunderstanding. But the bones are there.

This is a manual for a course Rick developed for Canadian police. As such, it deals with one very dangerous problem — knife defense. If you've ever faced a blade, you know it's a desperate fuckin' problem. There are no sure answers. When you survive, mentally it's because of your decision. Physically, it is because you were more efficient than the man with the better weapon. You used time, space and motion better than the guy who should have won.

In this very simple book about a very simple technique, Rick goes deep into what efficiency means. The principles that underlie everything that work are the same, whether we call the system ancient, classical, traditional or modern. And Rick understands and can explain those principles as well as anyone I know.

— Rory Miller Portland, OR 22June2017

Rory Miller is the author of *Mediations on Violence*, *Facing Violence*, *Scaling Force*, and many more excellent resources for those of us interested in self-defence.

# How to use this book / manual

It is more appropriate to refer to this document as a manual rather than a book.

The goal is to give you a tool and guide to work through learning self defence against a knife, a difficult topic where there are no firm answers just better options.

I wrote the manual because many many years ago a good friend, Reg Kinal, and I were in the dojo one morning and we found some rubber tanto training knives. We thought, "Hey we're black belts, how hard could knife defence be" so we attacked each other. The good thing about those rubber knives when they are new is that they leave black marks on a white Karate gi. Within a very short period of time we were covered in black lines and had "died" over and over again.

We learned two things:
1. We had no idea how to defend against a knife. We were trained but not trained.
2. Arrogance will get you killed. Even though we were black belts, if you haven't trained in something then you know crap about it.

From that day on I set out to find a knife defence system that would give me and others a chance to survive.

There wasn't a lot out there in the beginning or even now that fit everything into one solid teachable piece and didn't require learning an entirely new martial art.

After years of study and searching and trial and error I found a system that works well at all distances of attack and can be taught.

Empty hand against a knife is difficult. There are no easy absolute answers. Anyone who claims there is, is full of it. I wanted something that increased my odds of surviving, that gave me a fighting chance. There was a large void and that void still exists.

That is the purpose of this manual, to fill that void.

This book mirrors the seminar where I teach the knife defence system and walks through the drills in the order they should be done for the best learning experience.

The value of this manual is in working from start to finish because there is a progressive learning of skills and principles built into the order of this manual.

Pay attention to the principles explained in each drill and what we want to achieve with them, because those are what will make it all work.

There are two types of drills in the Manual: Training Drills where a new element or skill is learned and Practice Drills (Operant Conditioning Drills) where those elements and skills are practiced.

Keep prominent in your mind that:
- Training is for Learning.
- Practice is for Function.

What I mean by this is, in the Training Drills I want you to take your time and do everything as described but also understand why you are doing it. Stopping in the middle of a movement in training to understand if you are in the strategic spot you should be is okay, because you are learning.

In Practice, you don't do anything you don't want to do in a real situation (i.e. stop before being safe, hand the knife back for another rep or help the bad guy up). In Practice, we are going for things to work. The principles are important. If a successful move had the principles but didn't look much like what was described for Training, so what? The success of the principles was more important.

# Introduction

This manual is about defending from any edged or stabbing weapon attack, but for simplicity I will refer to the weapon as a knife.

The knife is a common weapon on Canadian (and other) streets today. It can maim and, more importantly, it can kill.

While the best defence against this dangerous attack is to leave the situation, we all know that is not always an option. You may not be given the chance to leave, you may have others to protect, or, for members of law enforcement or security, you may have a duty not to leave.

Understanding that a knife assault is deadly is the first step in achieving the main goal: your survival.

Understanding that it is the person wielding the knife who will harm you is the second step in achieving your goal. The person is the threat: stop the person and you stop the threat. A knife laying on the ground cannot harm you. Once it is picked up, the person holding it can.

Dealing with a knife is dangerous. In empty hand vs. empty hand a mistake means getting hit, but with a knife it means getting cut or stabbed.

This manual is all about learning to deal with a knife. As with all learning, it is done in progressive steps with each step dealing with more complex and difficult subjects than the last.

The foundations of defending yourself will be established progressively via defending against assault from large distances, and will be adapted as the distance of the assault gets closer and the attacks are more real.

My approach to teaching is most often principle based vs. techniques based, which makes this book seem like a departure. If someone comes to me knowing how to strike, then I can add principles to his foundation to help them strike harder. This book is very principle based; however, it also delivers the foundation, or technique, for knife defence. As you will see the foundation is designed to eliminate alternative actions which can create a freeze from indecision or simply too many options. I need to put the foundation in place to attach the principles that make this all work effectively and efficiently.

Even though I am giving a framework, always look for "why." If I say step here like this, why? If I say put your arms here, why? The key to making things work when all hell is breaking loose is the "why." If you know why, then you can find some way to make that happen and even if it doesn't look like the perfect form done in a safe training environment it doesn't matter. The why makes it work. In everything presented here work to understand the why.

In this book we will use the following terms:

- The person attacking with the knife shall be called **the Aggressor**.
- The person protecting themselves from the knife shall be called **the Respondent**.

We begin with the foundation principles in large movements and build as we cover the following:

- Attacks from at least one large step away.
- Attacks from an arm's reach away.
- Attacks from within one foot away.
- Assassinations where the non-weapon arm is used to attempt to control you:
  - To grab your clothing
  - To hook behind your head
  - As a brace, and other forms of grabbing/holding, to hold you away from the weapon arm
- Shaking your hand
- A tough overhand stab

We will also deal with Situations where the Aggressor has closed on you and is holding the blade on you to get your compliance:
- Knife on body: front, side back, etc.
- Knife to throat from front
- Knife to throat from behind

We will end where the Aggressor is at large distance and threatening with the blade. You can respond with:
- Empty hand
- Baton
- Improvised weapons

# Training: Safety First

Before you begin any training, you need to have the right equipment. Training knives come in various forms: foam, plastic, wood, metal, and even ones that deliver a shock.

I do not recommend using real knives. The chance of injury or death is too great. While training with a live blade adds realism and does get you used to seeing that flash of metal, so will a metal trainer.

Even though the appearance of a live blade adds realism, I do not believe any of the attacks will be pushed to a "real" level of intensity, because unless you are training with a sociopath, your partner will never attack you with intent for fear of harming you. (Besides, good luck talking to your insurance company should an injury occur while using a live blade in training.)

The harder substance training knives work more realistically, in that they do not fold and you know when you have been cut or stabbed; however, there is an increased risk of injury if the attacks have true intent.

Shock training knives are now available and can eliminate false moves that can appear with rubber or dull training knives.

**Training Knives**

**Training and Real folder closed and open**

The trainer is dull and not as pointed, but it is still metal and can still injure which is why I like to use rubber trainers to teach and the metal only to practice. (I've put the little red training folder in the picture below an inch into an old phone book.)

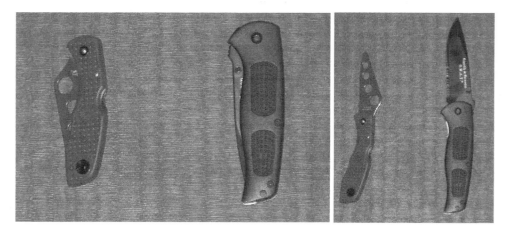

Another option is a homemade completely safe trainer (my preference when going hard). The trainer shown below is simply a gi belt folded and taped. Not flashy or cool but entirely safe, which is why when we go full out full speed we most often will use this cheap form of a trainer. I know my partner will not hold back because there is no way they can injure me with this safe training knife.

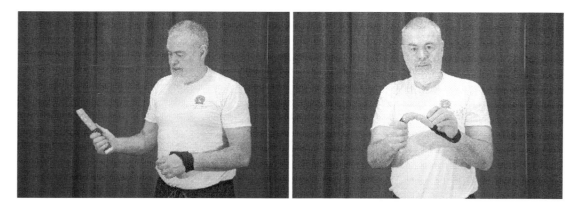

**Reality Note:** This may seem odd but I believe the most real attack and effective practice will come from training with the above totally safe training tool. The first reason is that the partner playing the Aggressor will have no hesitation going full out to stick that in you because they will not damage you. The second reason is that the partner playing the Aggressor will have no hesitation in going full out to stick that in you - NO THIS IS NOT A TYPO. Here's the thing, if I have a metal trainer then I know if I drive this into my partner in repeated sewing machine stabs full speed I will hurt them and very possibly damage them with broken ribs. Remember, I put that little red folding trainer an inch into an old phone book, so trust me when I say it could do damage to a human body. The human response is to avoid doing that damage but "look" like they are going hard and full out to stab but in fact they are pulling the knife back before it impacts the Respondent. Conscious or unconscious there is no intent to stab their partner. Martial artists know that a strike that is thrown just "to the body" and not "in the body" is distanced differently, even if that distance is just the length of the blade. In addition, humans like to succeed so if their intent is to stab you, even in a sewing machine fashion, they want to stab you. They expect to reach their target and feel some contact. That means if a body starts to move most humans will keep that stab going a little farther if they believe they can "get them," even though the "technique" is to strike and pull back quickly. There will be a story later about a person in a seminar being shocked that even knowing his partner was going to move, even seeing his partner moving he could not stop the stab. This is because the training tool was safe and he was really trying to stab his partner. NOT stabbing your partner is like a jab intended as a feint. If there is no intent to stab then there is no actual attack. Think about it, if you have repeatedly stabbed a partner in training with a hard plastic or metal training knife and they are still standing and not holding parts that are really hurting, then your training has a safety flaw of pulled attacks that cannot be responded to like a real attack. So, get a safe phoney training knife so you can attack for real.

**SAFETY NOTE:** You should also take great care to protect your eyes. There is various equipment you can use, depending on the level of protection required.

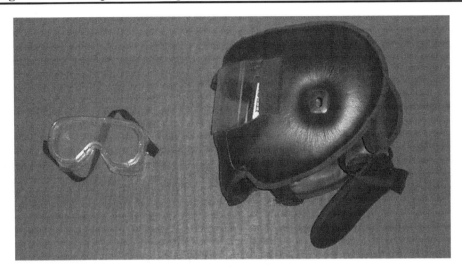

## Awareness

**Survival Note:** It is hard to survive the unexpected, so expect a weapon, look for a weapon. ALWAYS keep in mind there may be a weapon even when you can see their hands.

Knifings require close range and surprise for success. Often, your job may require you to be in close range. However, awareness can eliminate the element of surprise. Being aware and watchful for the deployment of a weapon is required.

## How to be Aware and of What

Glance at their hands.

There are many ways an Aggressor can stand holding a blade where even an experienced Respondent may not detect its presence. If you cannot see their palms, then you should assume they have a knife (or another weapon). If they keep their hands down by their belts, then you should assume they have a knife.

Most people talk with their hands in some way or at least have their hands in plain view. The more upset an Aggressor, the greater the likelihood that their hand movements will be more animated. Therefore, beware the calm person whose hands you cannot see.

As a counter point also beware the person who is demonstrating extremely animated hand movements. A skilled knife wielding Aggressor will capitalize on misdirection and distraction to achieve their end of harming you.

Look for:

- Hand out of sight at their side.

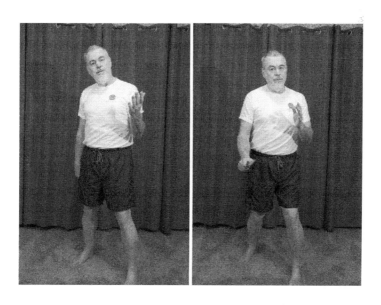

- Arms wrapped across their chest.

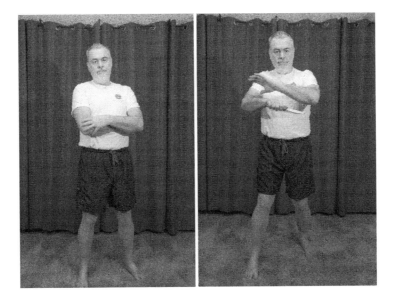

- Hand in their pocket.

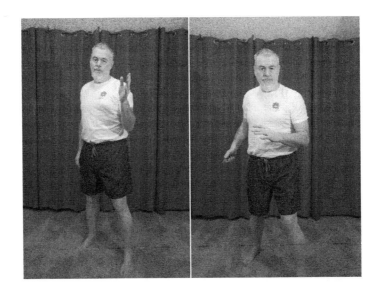

- Hands on their hips.

- Compulsive weapon check (touching to ensure weapon is in place). Knives can be secreted in any location on the body. A "knife fighter" will always have multiple knives at any given time. (A knife doesn't have to be large to harm you. The blade used in an autopsy is an inch long.)
- On a windy day, holding the shirt edge down so it does not blow up to reveal a weapon.

And many more.

If you cannot see their hands, then the safest course is to assume there is a weapon.

Once you have glanced at their hands, keep strong eye contact to give the clear message you are prepared to deter that sucker punch (same thing with a knife). Do not be distracted. Maybe another split-second glance back at their hands could be needed if you feel they have shifted. Use your peripheral vision to watch for a movement indicating deploying a weapon.

If you find looking the Aggressor directly in the eyes too hard to do without being intimidated by them, then look right between their eyes. This will give you the same peripheral vision and they will see it as you looking them dead in the eyes.

# Knife Attacks

Most knife attacks do not start with the Aggressor flashing the knife and giving you a chance to prepare yourself. Showing a weapon is for intimidation and is used to take control of a person (i.e. a process predator taking a person to sexually assault, torture and or murder).

Most knife attacks are knifings, which means they start up close and personal, and not from the distances usually displayed in movies.

- The Aggressor has the knife concealed and uses surprise.
- They do not want a fight; they just want to knife you.

Those in law enforcement and security will deal with individuals who conceal weapons and must be up close when intervention is required. You will not have distance between you and the Aggressor when the assault happens.

When they attack, they will use the non-weapon arm to either brace across your chest, grab your clothing or hook behind your head. While holding you they will attack with repeated stabs in a sewing machine fashion or with repeated slashes.

While the initial assault is most likely to happen from up close and personal, a distance attack can still happen if you propel the Aggressor away to either attempt to escape or obtain a weapon.

Sadly, as I am writing this manual, attacks with the Aggressor coming at you from a distance away are happening in terrorist attacks. So, while still not likely there is now a new scenario of possibility for an attack from a distance away.

**Reality Note:** It's not by accident that prison assassinations are all "sewing machine". Stabs are more lethal than slashes because it is harder for a medic to seal the wound or even know without imaging how deep the wound is. Although, Rory Miller says it may just be that sharpening a toothbrush into a point is easier than giving it an edge. (You can never be sure of the truthfulness of what inmates tell you.) In either case, the repeated stab is most often used. They also use opportunistic or cheap throw away knives, so they aren't concerned about losing the blade in your flesh.

### How the Knife Attacks

There are many systems describing angles of attack or lines of force. There are distinct angles a blade can come in and everything else is an alteration to one of those. For every angle except the straight stab at the centre point, there is an accompanying reverse slash or stab, so people who train with a knife also learn to reverse the direction of a slash with a stab and a stab with a slash.

For simplicity in training to defend against a knife I use Six Basic Attacks. The variety of angles that would increase the numbers are just a change in the angle of one of these Six Basic Attacks. The variations are endless but once you begin to learn to identify the incoming line of force, that is what you will be dealing with.

**Angles / Lines of Force: The Six Basic Knife Attacks**

- All movements will be described with the knife in the Aggressor's right hand, though all movements can also be done with the knife in the left hand.
- All movements can be done both with the edge of the blade (a cut), or the tip (a stab).
- All movements can be done with the knife held in a reverse grip (Knife held so that the blade extends down from the bottom of the hand with the cutting edge facing out.)

To help visualize the angles, picture the follow descriptions with the Aggressor facing you, blade in their right hand and a clock face imposed on their body. See the figure below the descriptions.

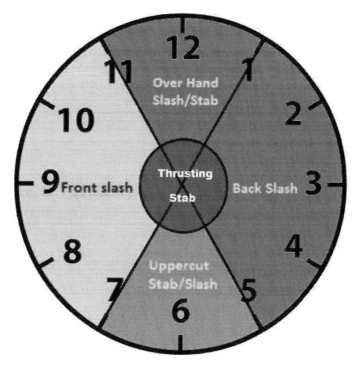

1.  **Thrusting Stab**: Thrust the blade straight forward with the point of the knife. The line of attack is the straight forward path of the point. Facing the Aggressor, blade comes out directly from the clock face.

**NOTE:** The most dangerous version of the thrusting stab is when the Aggressor uses their free hand to engage you as they stab repeatedly in a sewing machine like manner.

2. **Back Slash**: Bring the knife across your body from left to right. The line of attack is the arc the blade cuts through the air in front of the Aggressor. Facing the Aggressor, blade comes from between 1:00 and 5:00.

**NOTE:** The back slash from a reverse grip is done by turning the palm of the weapon arm upwards, thus turning the cutting edge of the blade towards the Respondent. The reverse grip can be used with the palm remaining down, however, it then becomes a back stab, but for defence it is treated the same as a back slash.

3. **Over Hand Slash/Stab**: With your right hand raised above your head strike straight down with the blade. The line of attack is the path straight down in front of the Aggressor. Facing the Aggressor, blade comes from between 11:00 and 1:00.

**NOTE:** Most often this is done as a stab with the knife held in some version of an icepick grip (see picture below), but larger blades such as a machete are often used in an over hand slash.

4. **Uppercut Stab/Slash**: While a cut can be done from this angle the easier movement is a stab coming up and possibly under a protective vest. Facing the Aggressor, blade comes from between 5:00 and 7:00.

5. **Front slash**: Bring the knife across your body from right to left. The line of attack is the arc the blade cuts through the air in front of the Aggressor. Facing the Aggressor, blade coming from between 7:00 to 11:00. (There is a "teaching" reason why this is #5 which will be covered later.)

6. **The Hack**: Done with a body rotation and by flicking the wrist so that the blade lashes out in a quick chopping motion. This is usually used when there is some distance between you and the Aggressor and they want to injure you or weaken you by cutting at your hands and limbs, so they can enter with more devastating strikes.

**Note:** Distance can be closed with surprising speed. In fact, the Tueller Rule was developed by Lt John Tueller who set up a drill where an armed suspect would rush an officer with a holstered firearm. He found that the suspect could close the distance and assault an average officer before they could draw and fire their weapon if they were within 21 feet. The way for the officer to adjust and survive is to move, adding distance and therefore adding time. More distance = more time.

While these are the main strikes, as stated before, there are numerous angles that they can be delivered from, thus making for numerous types of attacks. Thrusts can also be delivered from all of these angles. As the side slash comes from a higher and higher angle it becomes more like an overhand slash until it is one.

Once again please note, most knife attacks do not begin with the Aggressor flashing their knife. Most come from a quick stab or slash from a hidden from view knife.

Knife attacks, as with any violent assault or attempted ambush, do not always come from the front of you. In fact, if they truly wish to assassinate you, they will attack from an oblique angle or the rear.

**Survival Note:** The location of the hand you cannot see is a "tell" on the most likely angles of attack that might be used. To deviate from the most likely angle of attack they must reposition the knife. This gives you at least some potential intel on their next more.

What has been presented so far is how a knife assault happens. The other common use for knife before it is used in an assault is to get compliance. This is done by taking a person unaware and holding the knife on their body. These will be dealt with in the situation section.

## How to Stand When Defending Against a Knife

If you are aware you are interacting with the Aggressor, stand in a natural position with your feet about shoulder width apart and about the same distance as your normal step would be forming a bladed stance.

If you carry a weapon, stand with your weapons side back to discourage the Aggressor from attempting to grab your weapon. If you do not carry weapons (intended or improvised), then stand in whichever is your natural stance with one foot forward.

> **Skill Note:** As most knifings are surprises you may well find yourself in a neutral stance (feet side by side without one taking a forward position), therefore train from this stance as well.

Your arms should be raised and turned so the backs of your forearms face the Aggressor, this protects the vulnerable veins on the underside of the forearms. You can talk with your hands to obtain this position in a non-threatening manner. You can take the "Jack Benny" position. You can have your arms laid across your front, but NOT crossed or interlaced in any way. Find a natural non-aggressive position for your arms to be up and useful.

From this position, if necessary, you can quickly turn the bottom or top of the forearm to meet the blade while still protecting the vulnerable inside of the forearm and trying to protect the muscle and tendons of the outer forearm. Severed tendons can result in the loss of the use of your hands.

We do not stand with the bone facing the Aggressor because a quick hack may get to the inside of the forearm before we can turn the arm to meet it.

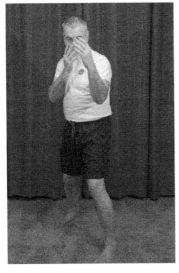 

Never interlace your arms as seen below. You cannot move them quickly and they are easily pinned to your body:

Instead of interlacing fold them on top of each other which allows them to be easily moved and difficult to pin:

Another position is called the Jack Benny Stance named after a famous old time variety show host who stood with his arms like the picture below. This position allows again for quick use of the arms:

PLEASE NOTE THAT YOU SHOULD NEVER VOLUNTEER TO TAKE A CUT. I AM NOT SUGGESTING THAT YOU PURPOSELY BLOCK A BLADE WITH YOUR FLESH. HOWEVER, A SLICED FOREARM IS PREFERABLE TO A CUT THROAT.

There is one overriding law of knife defence:

YOU WILL BE CUT AND YOU WILL BLEED!

Know it and expect it.

You are facing a sharp, edged weapon. Whether it is a knife, razor or broken bottle, you will be cut. How badly, and where you are cut, you can control.

To help prepare yourself, visualize a knife attack with yourself being cut (badly cut) AND continuing to a successful defence.

If you get cut and let yourself go into a freeze, you will not see the next strike and it will be the one that kills you. This is exactly what the experienced knife fighter is trying to do with their short slashes and hacks.

When you practice, never stop just because you would have been cut.

There are some who believe stating this distinct possibility upfront is a negative perspective and perhaps even damaging to the survival mindset. While I respect our difference of opinion, I disagree. I believe that being mentally prepared to continue even if cut is a strength of purpose that far out weighs any negative perspective. Being mentally prepared to be cut may prevent a freeze.

## Of course, if you don't get cut then it was a good day.

**Survival Note:** If you know you are dealing with a potential Aggressor, either as a civilian dealing with an upset person or as law enforcement/security interviewing someone, you should always be in a blade stance and slightly off line from the Aggressor's centre line.

## What is a Drill?

What is the purpose of a drill?

- Drills are for training or practice.
- They are an artificial device to gain a specific skill.
- They are not real.

I hate when people look at a drill and say, "That's not real." Well, of course, it isn't. That is what the term artificial means: it is not real; it is a drill.

The reason for this section is that drills are needed. Understanding what a drill is and keeping the goal and purpose of a drill in mind and clear in teaching is important to avoid wavering from the path.

You need drills to train.

You should always know the skill sets being highlighted and trained in every drill that you do.

Always remember a drill is only a teaching tool. It is never real.

Always keep in mind that any drill is a cooperation between partners, no matter how energetic or intense you make it.

Do not let the cooperation lead you into the delusion that your training is somehow real fighting.

I included this section because there are a few issues I see people having with drills:

- People don't grasp it is artificial, therefore they toss it out when it isn't "real" and fail to gain the skill it would have taught.

- They don't know what the skill is they are supposed to learn therefore never achieve it, or the purpose of the drill is lost over time.
- They start to believe it is real and therefore slip into some fantasy world of delusion.

# DRILL: Attack with the Knife

**Purpose:** This drill should bring home how dangerous a knife attack is and the fact that distance is your friend. The partner being attacked is to observe the incoming attack and observe the difference in the attacks as the distance gets closer.

**Distance = Time = Opportunity**

One partner takes a defensive stance. You are the meat puppet; your role is to stand there and be a living dummy and do NOTHING. This is a drill: you not moving isn't real, but you will learn things.

**STEP ONE:** One partner has the knife, the Aggressor, and from a distance that requires at least **one large step** to close the distance they move in as fast as they can SAFELY run through the Six Basic Attacks (including the Hack).

Thrusting Stab:

Back Slash:

Over Hand Stab:

Uppercut Stab:

Front Slash:

The Hack:

**STEP TWO:** The Aggressor from a distance that is **an arm's length**, as fast as they can SAFELY run through the first five of the Six Basic Attacks. (The Hack is a distance attack.)

Thrusting Stab:

Back Slash:

Over Hand Stab:

Uppercut Stab:

Front Slash:

**STEP THREE:** The Aggressor from a distance that is **within one foot**, as fast as they can SAFELY run through the first five of the Six Basic Attacks. (The Hack is a distance attack.)

Thrusting Stab:

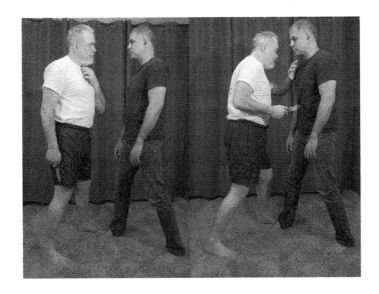

Back Slash:

Over Hand Stab:

Uppercut Stab:

Front Slash:

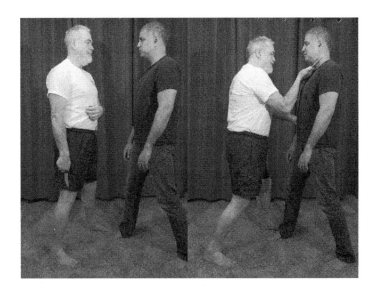

**STEP FOUR:** The Aggressor with their non-weapon arm grab their partner's (The Respondent) clothing for control. With the weapon arm, using a sewing machine-like stabbing action perform repeated stabs.

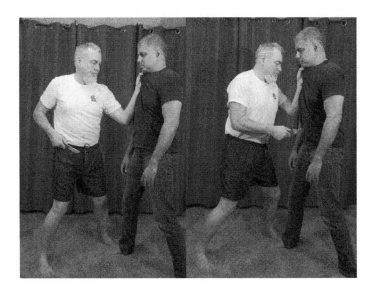

**STEP FIVE:** The Aggressor with their non-weapon arm cup the back of the Respondent's head for control. With the weapon arm, using a sewing machine-like stabbing action perform repeated stabs.

**STEP SIX:** The Aggressor with their non-weapon arm brace it across the Respondent's body to hold them off and control and use a sewing machine-like stabbing action perform repeated stabs.

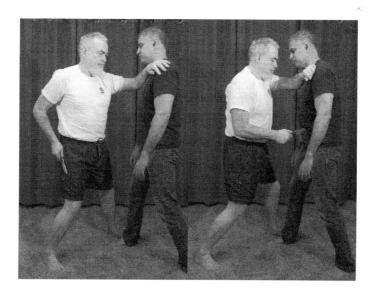

**STEP SEVEN:** The Aggressor has the knife in their left hand, they offer their right to shake hands. When the hand shake happens, they pull the Respondent in and slip towards their back, and using a sewing machine-like stabbing action perform repeated stabs to their back.

**STEP EIGHT:** This one comes from the research done by Randy King of KPC Self Defence in Edmonton, Alberta. A style of assault becoming common is the overhand stab, but the Aggressor keeps their elbow tight to the body as they stab in a short sewing machine manner.

Change which partner has the knife and repeat.

Working this drill at speed will show how much more dangerous and difficult to deal with the closer attacks are and how the Aggressor using their non-weapon arm to interfere with you makes it even more difficult, and therefore why we have to build our skills before dealing with those difficult attacks.

The sewing machine attack is the most dangerous and very common. We will deal with those attacks last.

# Why would we deal with large movements first when smaller movements are more likely and more dangerous?

How do we learn to hit a baseball?

The average speed of a major-league fastball is over 90 mph. If you want to play in the big league you will need to know how to hit a fast ball.

We don't start learning to hit a ball going over 90 mph. You must build the skills from something simpler and work up to it.

We will use the same approach, giving you distance and therefore time and the opportunity to learn, BUT we will, by the end, deal with the sewing machine attack.

In learning to deal with the large movements, we learn the principles to deal with knife assaults. We lay the foundation for what is going to be needed to deal with the smaller deadlier attacks.

As the knife assaults shrink in size and movement, so will our response alter, adapt and shrink to deal with them, but the underlying principles learned in the large movements will carry through and remain.

The Aggressor's large attacks with a knife adapt and alter when they become smaller, but are basically the same and so it will be with our responses.

This approach is also why until the end the Aggressor will be in front of you. You need to learn to see and learn to respond. Having the Aggressor in front makes that easier for people to learn. We will end with the Aggressor coming from the side.

But before we begin to train we need to know what to train and that requires planning. To plan you need to know your Goals, Strategy, Tactics and Techniques.

# Goals, Strategy, Tactics and Techniques

(Concepts used with permission from Rory Miller)

- You need to do some thinking ahead of any encounter.

- You need to consider facing a person with a knife.

- You need to know what you want to do based on the totality of circumstances.

- Visualization exercises are a great way to begin to prepare and know what you want to do.

- Training and practicing what you have determined is also required.

- Of course, all good plans last right up to the first engagement. As Mike Tyson said, "Everyone has a plan until they get punched in the face." But you need a framework to work from rather than floundering in indecision.

## How do we plan ahead?

A good friend from whom I have learned a tremendous amount is Rory Miller. Rory presents a method for determining how to approach thinking and planning for self-defence.

In his book "Meditations on Violence: A Comparison of Martial Arts Training & Real World Violence" on page 30 Rory writes:

1. Goals dictate strategy.
2. Strategy dictates tactics.
3. Tactics dictate techniques.

I love how Rory breaks things down and this is an excellent example.

To understand this approach, we need to understand the terms.

- **Goal:** What you want to achieve, the object of your efforts, your end game.
- **Strategy:** Literally defined as "The Art of War," strategy is the planning of movement into favourable positions.
- **Tactics:** The calculated procedure of engaging the enemy to gain some end.
- **Techniques:** The mechanical skill to achieve one's ends.

In planning ahead, you must work logically from your goal to the potential strategies to definitive tactics to workable techniques.

**Planning**

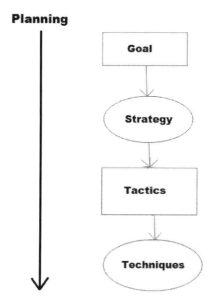

## Why know and understand your strategy?

More detail to come, but simply put, it is easier to alter a plan than to make one. If you already know your goal then you can start to formulate your strategy (your plan) to achieve it.

If you have a plan you must have some idea how to get it done: tactics.

Once you have the tactics you can figure out the nitty gritty, get dirty, realities needed to get it done: your techniques.

Knowing your goal and your strategy allows you to compare your tactics and see if they mesh with your strategy, that is, that the tactics you came up with will get you to your strategy and therefore your goal.

## Make sure your tactics = your strategy?

Randy King of KPC Self Defence in Edmonton says, "No one runs away doing Jujitsu."

Let me dissect that quote to show how the tactic chosen meant the strategy they wanted failed:

- Goal = survive
- Strategy = run away (escape)
- Tactic = Jujitsu
- Technique = grappling with the Aggressor (lock, choke etc.)

BUT how do you run away while you have a hold of the Aggressor?

Therefore, you can't run away, so "No one runs away doing Jujitsu." (Yes, if I use a throw to propel someone away from me then I can run, but you get the point I am trying to make.)

If your strategy was to escape, then grapping was not the right tactic.

**Your tactic and technique did not match up to your strategy of escape, therefore, you failed to reach your goal.**

This failure could result in a hesitation, an indecision or a complete freeze.

In application, there must be a logical flow back from the techniques used to enact your tactics to achieve your strategies to get to your goal.

**How your Goal / Strategy / Tactics / Techniques = How and What You Should Train**

Understanding your goal and your strategy will also direct your training.

While you always want to train for all contingencies if the strategy you want to rely on most is to distance and deploy a baton, then training should be heavier in how to disengage and deploy.

Absolutely you want to train control and disable, but operant conditioning kicks in fast and if you trained 70% of the time to go for control, then going for control is more likely what you will do.

Do your thinking now.

Visualize scenarios and what would be the best strategy, what tactics will that mean, and therefore what techniques you need to train.

Don't get distracted by what is more fun. Controlling and disabling are fun to practice, but if your strategy is escape then you must work on the tactics to achieve that strategy.

# Goal: Survival

I am going to work from the premise that your main goal is to survive the assault. I don't believe that is an incorrect assumption for sane people.

A secondary goal may be to fulfill your employment obligations (if you have them).

A secondary goal may be protecting others or citizens.

But unless you survive you cannot meet either secondary goal. Therefore, again, your survival is the priority goal.

## The Four Strategies for Survival

### Citizens

The following strategies to achieve your goal of survival are listed in the preferred order for citizens. The preferred order is going from the least risk to the highest risk. Circumstance, situation, environment, obligation and luck will determine which you attempt.

1. Escape
2. Distance and deploy weapon
3. Disable
4. Control

### Law Enforcement and Security

Your Duty to Engage as an LEO or security may require the strategies to be listed differently by placing escape at the bottom, because you cannot leave, and control before disable, even though disable would be safer for you. However, your primary goal of survival should not be placed at risk. The knife is a lethal weapon and most people don't realize that until confronted by a determined attacker armed with one. Always remember that a valid reason for upping the use of force is the fact you're losing. Control can shift to disable when it is the only option for your survival. Also, escape may be rephrased as going for backup.

1. Distance and deploy weapon
2. Control
3. Disable
4. Escape

Understand that as in all things there are no guarantees. Everything depends on the totality circumstance: situation, environment, your ability, the ability of the Aggressor, any injuries you have obtained, and luck.

If you look at the strategies, you can see they will dictate what you want to do.

If you want to distance and deploy a weapon, then you do not want to grab onto the Aggressor. That makes it hard to put distance between you and them.

If you need to disable them, then committing both your arms to pinning them to the ground cannot be the end game, you must injure them.

Let's look at the strategies.

# Escape

**Survival Note:** If you are not there you cannot get stabbed.

Putting space between you and the Aggressor is your first line of defence.

Space/distance = time = opportunity. This will be repeated because it is important.

If possible, leave the area and move to a safer area (populated, etc.).

If possible, place an object between you and the Aggressor.

If the surprise attack comes and you cannot yet initiate the defence of escape, then engage and propel the Aggressor away to give you enough time to escape.

Escape can give time to call for back up or, if a citizen, call law enforcement.

# Distance and Deploy a Weapon or Obtain an Improvised Weapon

**Survival Note:** Do not let arrogance get you killed. No matter how good you get in going empty hand vs. knife, no matter how confident you are, one mistake could be your last. Whenever possible arm yourself to go against a knife.

To deploy or grab an improvised weapon, you must gain distance, which will give you the time and opportunity to deploy and use a weapon.

To gain distance, you cannot become entangled with the Aggressor.

You want distance, therefore, if possible get it immediately without engaging with the Aggressor.

If it is not possible (for example, you're jumped), then your strategy is to disengage in a manner that gains as much distance as you can (propel the Aggressor away from you).

If you carry a weapon (i.e. law enforcement or security), when circumstance and situation allow, you should always distance and then deploy your weapon when facing a knife.

A knife is lethal force, therefore, if you carry a lethal force weapon this is your best option PROVIDED you have the time to deploy. (Always refer to your operational procedures.)

The next best weapon is one that gives you a distance over the knife: a baton, long flashlight or stick.

Flexible weapons that give distance are the next choice: a belt, rope, cord or chain, even a backpack or purse. A good friend of mine, David Elkin's Wing Chun Sifu, survived a bar parking lot assault by using his bomber jacket as a whip with the zipper as the tip. He targeted the eyes which scared off an Aggressor.

Anything else to increase the impact or penetration (even a pen) is the next step.

If you need to grab an improvised weapon, **make sure you have identified** what you want to grab, where it is, and how to get to it. Don't end up standing looking around.

# Disable

Disable is a safer option than control because it should end the threat. Ending the threat is easier than trying to maintain control over the threat.

The knife is a lethal weapon, therefore the amount of force that can be used is considerable.

To disable the Aggressor, you need to be close.

You need to be fully committed to the intended damage. You cannot hesitate. Disable through an arm break or multiple strikes or driving them forcefully into the ground.

# Control

Control requires you to get your hands on the Aggressor. Luckily if they are attempting to knife you they will come to you.

Control must be absolute. Go for control fully committed, because any hesitation leaves openings and opportunities for the Aggressor.

Once control is gained the Aggressor must be placed in a position that makes it exceptionally hard for them to escape your control.

Controlling a person is best achieved with solid body mechanics and proper use of rotation, leverage, shearing, empty space, and gravity. These concepts will be explained soon.

**NOTE:** This book will not address distancing to deploy a firearm for Law Enforcement or a person with a legal carry permit. That is both beyond the scope of the text and my training; however, I wanted to include here a note that when an Officer distances and deploys a firearm the next step is to order the subject to comply with dropping the weapon. That is a form of taking control and only when the strategy of control fails do they move to the next strategy of disable (disable can include lethal force).

# The Tactics of Knife Defence

The Tactics of knife defence are the step by step approach required to survive and get to one of the Four Strategies for Survival.

There are two sets of Tactics, because your strategy will determine your tactics.

We have four strategies: Escape, distance and deploy weapon, disable, and control.

Escape, Distance and deploy weapon require tactics where you are distancing yourself away from the Aggressor.

Disable and Control require tactics where you are closing with the Aggressor.

Therefore, we have two sets of tactics:

## A) Distancing Tactics for Escape or Distance and Deploy a Weapon

    **1) Avoid while intercepting the attack**

    **2a) Propel the Aggressor away from you**

    **3a) Stop the threat: escape or deploy weapon**

> **Survival Note:** While it may be obvious, if you can escape or distance and deploy without engaging the Aggressor that is the first option. The above set is when you must engage before escaping or deploying a weapon.

## B) Closing Tactics for Disable or Control

    **1) Avoid while intercepting the attack**

    **2b) Control lunge step and take control of the weapon arm**

    **3b) Stop the threat: control or disable**

Fortunately, the first Tactic in both sets is the same and is the same for a very important reason, one that forms the foundation of this approach to dealing with a knife assault: the fact we have a natural response to a knife coming at us.

The chart below shows how to move through from Goal to Strategy to Tactics.

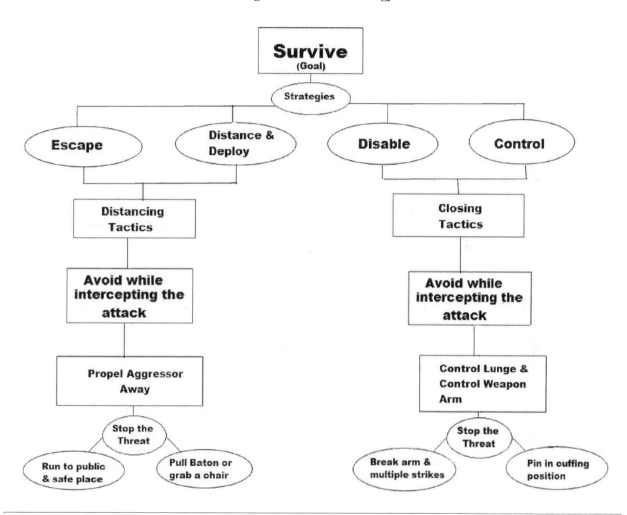

**Teaching Note:**

Avoid while intercepting the attack is the critical tactic to get right. It is the same first tactic in the Distancing Tactics and the Closing Tactics. It is composed of two vital pieces fitted together but to fit them properly you need to start with the first piece alone: avoid the attack. Then add in "while intercepting."

Once that has been done there are a few ways to choose to teach and it will depend on your audience. You can take one attack and work it all the way through Distancing Tactics and Closing Tactics or you work all attacks through Distancing tactics before taking on Closing Tactics. That is my preferred choice.

> **Teaching Note:**
> Keep your audience in mind. If you are teaching civilians you want to focus on Stopping the Threat by Escape or Disable but not control because it isn't an obligation for citizens. You do want to cover distancing and deploying a weapon and spend some time on control in case they need it, for example they may not wish to disable a disturbed child/family member, but it shouldn't be the focus.

If you are teaching law enforcement or security personnel who have a duty to control the Aggressor then spend a good amount of time on control but still cover disable because if you are losing you need to give up on control and move to disable (or propel away) to stay safe.

This system of knife defence is based on two fundamental elements. First, I believe there is a natural, universal response to a sharp weapon assaulting you; therefore, that is where we start and the second element is that the system is built on a foundation of solid principles.

## Everything Starts with the Natural Response

### "You can't fight natural instinct, but you can make natural instinct fight for you." William Fairbain.

The design of this system is based off a very natural instinctive reaction to being attacked with a sharp pointy weapon.

Fear is a natural reaction to danger and is always in your best interest. It is your natural warning siren. Always pay attention to feelings of fear. I used to label this the Natural Fear Response, but have recently changed to a very appropriate name: **The OCR which stands for The Oh Crap Response**.

Basically, the body, mind and spirit have the same reaction to a sharp edged pointy weapon trying to do them damage: fear. The body, mind and spirit know the knife can hurt them so they rightfully fear and respect the blade and actively move the body away from the attack, throwing the arms up and out to protect the body from the blade and to help withdraw the body from the line of attack.

In this system, not only do we not fight the OCR, we accept it and we encourage it. If the natural reaction is to pull the body away from the knife and throw our arms out in a structure to intercept the knife and that is what the body wants then that is what we will do.

We will tinker with it to make it an effective movement. Again, because we are working with the most instinctive reaction of the body, mind and spirit to protect ourselves, most people learn this system very quickly.

Because we want you to learn apply this natural movement in a tactical manner when we start it will seem less natural but the closer the attack, the more we will reflect and call upon that natural movement.

The OCR as a starting point to adapt to an operant conditioned response has been taught for many years by many people under many names. Moshe Feldenkrais was teaching it back in the 1930's.

**Because we naturally move our bodies out of the way of the knife and throw our arms between us to prevent the knife from getting closer the first tactic in both the Distancing Tactics and the Closing Tactics will be: Avoid while intercepting the attack.**

# Principles Make Techniques Work

There are some very important concepts that make everything work. I am going to list and briefly describe these concepts but they will be described further as we use them. For the purpose of this manual I am going to call them all principles. The principles are what you need to take away from this study to make things work in chaos. Take a moment to think these over and watch for them to be used as we learn how to apply the tactics. There is a lot here but don't panic, I just want you to have an idea of what I am talking about when we put these into action.

1. **Move YOU not THEM:** Most of the time it is easier to move us than to move the Aggressor and often when we do we also affect their structure.

2. **Empty Space:** Using empty space is the key to not fighting force on force. If you think of a person standing and you place your hand on top of their shoulder and press directly down you can picture that press will have little effect. It has little effect because you are pressing into the person's body (their

structure). Directly behind the person's shoulder is — nothing. No other body parts. No structure. The space behind their shoulder is empty. If we press their shoulder into that Empty Space we will have an effect on their body. We use empty space in movement too. If you were trying to catch an elevator and the doors were almost closed you would angle your body and slide through the open space between the doors. You would never think of trying to bash through the doors to get in. We apply the same approach when we move dealing with an Aggressor.

3. **Rotation:** Rotation will be used a great deal in this system because it adds a spiral action which is powerful.

4. **Structure:** This is our skeletal frame work which we want aligned so that it can withstand incoming pressure and support outgoing force. Everything comes from structure and everything goes into structure. A properly aligned skeleton allows us to use as little muscle as needed to remain in position. This means we have more muscle available to move quickly (no change in use) it allow allows us to stay loose (see below).

5. **Arms are MOVED not Moving:** We want to use our whole body when we move to increase power. If we just move our arms around then all we have is arm strength. If we use our body rotation to move our arms then we use whole body power. The arms will bend and unbend, rotate, and expand but if we want our arm to move to the right with power we do it by rotating our body to the right.

6. **Loose:** Tensing inhibits movement and never improves anything. Stay loose.

7. **Tendon Power:** I call this tendon power but your body is really a big ball of elastic, not only tendons but particularly your fascia, and accessing that elasticity allows you to access the natural springs of the body to increase acceleration and power.

8. **Leverage:** Because the body is made with things sticking out from the torso we have many options to use as levers to pry the torso to where we want it.

9. **Shearing:** Use to manipulate the Aggressor's structure by cutting through part of their body with an edge of yours (forearm, wrist bone, shin etc.) It applies an oblique angled force, like a wedge, to increase the effectiveness of pressing on the Aggressor's body.

10. **Control the Distance:** Distance is the space between you and the Aggressor. You want to determine how much space between you exists. The kick boxing legend, Joe Lewis, used to say fights are won by the guy controlling the distance.

11. **Balance:** In Jigoro Kano's book "Kodokan Judo" before every throw is described they instruct you to take the opponent's balance. Basically, to knock a person down you must take their balance. Therefore, if you are out of balance you have done all the work for your opponent and have set yourself up to be knocked down. Stay as balanced as you can by keeping your centre over your base (when standing your base is the space between your feet.)

12. **Move with your Centre:** Moving with your centre adds power, intent and maintains balance.

13. **Gravity:** We are going to use a principle called sinking by dropping our centre to affect the weapon arm by adding our mass to the action. Sinking is just a way to say using gravity to add to your mass. Gravity is free power and it is always there. Mass increases power. Think of the typical Karate Board break but using a baseball bat. Yes, the boards can be broken but if I change the bat out for a sledge hammer.... That is adding mass and when your mass is directly over what you want to drop it on then it can be done without effort. (You don't even have to lift the sledge.)

14. **Bone Slaving:** When we take possession of one of the Aggressor's body parts (i.e. Their Weapon Arm) we want to crush it to us, making their bones, their skeleton, our bones, our skeleton into ONE STRUCTURE so that when we move our skeleton theirs is moved too.

15. **Swallow:** To engulf, absorb, make disappear. I want you to think of an amoeba enveloping its food. If you are a horror movie fan think of the movie "Alien" where the alien rips out of the human's chest, only run the film backward sucking the alien in. BUT always remember it is done as you step.

16. **Smother:** To stifle, cover entirely, to suppress, to leave no room even for air. This is vital. You want to suck that weapon arm into to you as YOU move to it. Leave no room at all. Smother it into your chest. Like a vacuum-sealed bag, suck all the air out between you and the part of the Aggressor you are wanting to control. Think bone crushing to bone.

17. **Wringing out the towel:** Think of wringing the water out of a towel by grabbing each end and twisting in opposite directions: the weapon arm is your towel, wring it out. You want to synch out every millimetre of space between you and the weapon arm in a counter rotation.

18. **Elasticity:** Think of the old toy ball on the end of an elastic band: when you pull, it snaps towards you. It doesn't resist the band's pull, it travels with it. This is the mindset you must have to hold onto the Aggressor's weapon arm. If they pull the weapon arm and you resist, then the chances of them ripping free skyrocket. If, however, you go with them, then you neutralize their action. In all of this you are not being passive, you are moving on to the next tactic.

19. **Act in Motion:** Doing an action in motion almost always enhances the effect.

20. **Sticking, Adhering, Guiding and Leading:** We work at attaching sensors to the weapon arm (the CBI, explained later). We work hard at getting in contact with the weapon arm and the Aggressor. We want to attach immediately (stick). We want to stay attached (in Closing tactics) even as they move (adhere — sometimes called follow). We want to influence their movement (guide). We want to encourage them to go where we want them to (lead). To guide and particularly to lead require real intent from your training partners to show their effectiveness.

21. **Never Alarm the Aggressor:** This principle comes from a Tim Cartmell book. If you alarm the Aggressor then they know you are doing something or they know what they are doing is failing and they

change. Now you have something new to deal with. Think of a pickpocket, when they are lifting a wallet or watch they absolutely do not want to alarm their target. Only once the pickpocket is long gone do they realize what has happened and it is too late. Simply put, if you share your plan it is no longer any good.

Again, while this seems like a lot of things to be doing they are done with simple body movements and will be easy to accomplish in our techniques.

# The Nitty, Gritty, Down and Dirty of How to Action the Tactics = Techniques

Remember the first Tactic is the same for both Distancing Tactics and Closing Tactics, so the following applies to BOTH sets of tactics.

We know the tactics we want to use to employ our strategies, now we need the tools to make it happen, our techniques. But remember techniques must be done with our principles.

**NOTE:** The first time I introduce how to do something I am going to go into a lot of detail. I want to be clear on what is to be done and how. I do not know who is reading this right now, what your training or experience is, so the first time I am going to explain as if the reader is just starting out on this journey we all love so much.

1. **Avoid while intercepting the attack**

**Piece 1: Avoid the Attack**

Avoiding the attack requires movement.

Movement is the key to your survival.

This is THE most important concept in this system.

Moving to avoid the attack:

- Keeps you alive.
- Gives you a strategic positioning.
- Allows you to engage the Aggressor with you in control of how that happens.
- Makes everything to follow work.

The reason all the pictures have me in a T-shirt and shorts rather than a cool tactical outfit is so that you can clearly see my legs, where and how they are moved. Movement is that important. (Even more important than me looking cool. Plus, I usually wear jeans not tactical pants.)

Each angle of the blade's attack represents a line of force. The concept of avoiding the attack is simple: get off the line of force.

Of course, execution of this concept is often harder. The smaller the movement of the knife, and the higher the skill of the Aggressor, the greater the risks. Which is why, when learning, we begin with the larger movement attacks.

There is a specific easy method of stepping that increases the efficiency and effectiveness of the techniques you will be employing. Before we do anything else, learning these simple steps may save your life.

I will be very detailed below about how to move but always keep in mind it is just stepping and you've been doing that almost all your life.

# DRILL: Skill Set #1: Movement

**Purpose:** To learn an efficient and effective way to move.

- The simplicity of this stepping movement is that all you must do is move your feet forward in a straight line **and** rotate your hips and feet as you complete every step.
- The feet are your **BASE** and must remain under you for stability.
- The efficiency and effectiveness are added by the rotation of your hips/centre.
- The rotation of your hips/centre is your **POWER GENERATOR**.

In usage, which foot do I step forward with?

You want to rotate to the open side.

If your right foot is forward the rotation is to the open side to your left.

If your left foot is forward the rotation is to the open side to your right.

The foot you step forward with dictates which is the open side. This will be clearer once we begin to apply the steps and rotations.

1. **Sliding Hip Rotation Step:**

   - Your lead foot moves forward first.

   - The trailing (back) foot catches up to the lead foot.

   - Your feet move in **a straight line** to your objective.

   - **AS** your lead foot touches the ground use your hips to rotate on the ball of the foot.

   - Your back foot catches up returning you to a stable stance.

   - You can see from the diagram below rotating on the balls of your feet moves your centre off line.

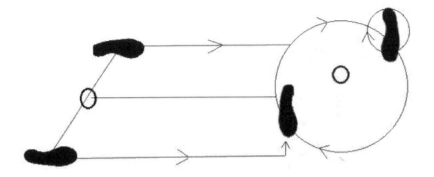

## 2. **Step Through Hip Rotation:**

- This is simply taking a normal but extended step moving the back foot through to the front to become the lead foot.
- Once you've stepped through, when covering distance, the back foot then catches up to the lead foot to bring you back into stance.
- Your feet move in **a straight line** to your objective.
- **AS** your (now) lead foot touches the ground use your hips to rotate on the ball of the foot.
- Again, note the shift in your centre's position in the diagram below.

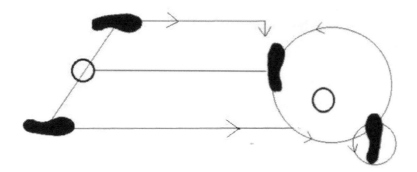

**View with rotation ending facing the front:**

### 3. Rotation:

- Rotate your hips so you turn 90 degrees on the balls of your feet.
- This is a rotation about an axis (the centre of your body) with one side going forward and one side going backwards. (This is an important point for the manipulation of a person's structure.)
- Rcpcat to facc thc other direction if desired.
- The diagram below shows the shift in your centre's position.

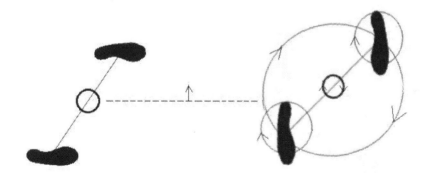

When you move stay balanced, keep your feet (your base) under you.

**Teaching Notes:** When I teach these movements, I have the students move across the room in front of me (open side towards me) and at the end of the movement they must be FACING me. If they are not facing me then we all know they failed to rotate at the end of the step. This rotation is vital not only for avoiding the attack and power generation but also because it also places us in a strategic position allowing us to make use of empty space rather than going force on force. Using the rotation also incorporates the entire body rather than just upper body strength.

Run through each of the movements from both left and right stances ensuring you have completely rotated at the end of the movement.

# Drill: Skill Set #2: Movement — Getting off the line of force

**Purpose:** To learn how the movement just practiced is used to get off the line of force.

The principle we want to be taken away here is that **it is easier to move you rather than them** so ALL actions defending against a knife require you to move YOU.

The movement you will make to get off the line of force will not only depend on the angle but of the size of the movement.

Whenever possible, it is better to be on the outside of the weapon arm because it limits the Aggressor's options to respond.

The rotation is the key and vital once the attacks get smaller.

**Inside or Outside of the Weapon arm**

If your partner stands and holds their arms out in front of them and you are not between their extended arms you are in the Outside of the weapon arm position.

Outside Weapon Arm:

If your partner stands and holds their arms out in front of them and you are inside of the extended arms (in between them) you are in the Inside of the weapon arm position.

Inside Weapon Arm:

Whenever possible end on the outside of the weapon arm, as it leaves the Aggressor less offensive options than when you are inside the weapon arm.

We will work solely on the first part of "Avoid while intercepting the Attack": Avoid the Attack in this drill.

We will deal with the "Hack" in a separate section.

All descriptions are with the Aggressor in a left foot forward stance, holding the knife in their right hand. Train both sides (we will explain preparing for left handed Aggressors in a later section).

All descriptions are with the Respondent in a left foot forward stance. Train both sides and train from a neutral stance.

NOTE: If you stand in a southpaw = right foot forward stance (I.e. Left handed so you keep your left weapon side back) then work from a right stance. However, it means where it says slide step you step through and where it says step through you slide step. This will allow you to rotate to the open side.

One partner, the Aggressor, holds the knife in their right hand in a saber grip (like you would hold a sword) and stands at least one large step away from the Respondent partner, just as in the "How to Attack with a Knife" drill, only this time the Respondent gets to move. The Respondent FOR THIS DRILL ONLY has their hands down, so that they can clearly see how their movement takes them off the line of attack.

## TECHNIQUE: Thrusting Stab

**Aggressor**: Steps through with their right foot to thrust at mid-level (stab at your partner's navel.)

**Respondent:** With their left foot slides straight forward and **rotates** to their right as their foot lands.

This movement will take them off the straight line of the attack and move them closer to the Aggressor.

The rotation means you will end facing 90 degrees to the weapon arm.

REPEAT this same movement in response to the: Back Slash, Overhand Stab and the Uppercut stab. This only gets you off the line it does not deal with the attack (that comes next).

For each of those attacks you need not change anything about how you move.

**NOTE THE PRINCIPLES**: The first principles we can see is that to avoid the knife we moved us not them. There was no need to get into a force on force contest to get out of the way. The second principle we used was empty space. The space beside the Aggressor is that space between the elevator doors. Again, this means we can move where we want without having to deal with the force or strength of the Aggressor. We also used rotation to get off the line of attack.

> **Teaching Notes:** One of the errors people make when stepping forward is they do not step straight and trust the rotation to avoid the knife (the intercept adds insurance next). Instead, they step out and away, placing them at the disadvantaged position of being too far away from the Aggressor to gain control or to damage immediately.
>
> The fix is to have them stand with a wall close enough on their left side preventing them from stepping out. Then they are forced to step straight.
>
> They will quickly see the improved positioning once they step properly.
>
> As an added benefit, they must rotate properly to avoid being stabbed.

# TECHNIQUE: Front Slash

The reason the Front Slash is dealt with last is because the angle of the attack requires you to move to the inside of the weapon arm and that makes your movement different from the one used for the other attacks.

**Aggressor**: Steps through with their right foot and cuts across their body at mid leave from right to left.

**Respondent:** With their right foot step through straight forward and **rotates** to their left as their foot lands.

You will see that against the large step and large movement attacks this stepping and rotating will get you off the line of the attack (inside the arc of the slash).

**NOTE THE PRINCIPLES:** I want you to start looking for the principles used in the techniques. Thinking back to the last "Note the Principles," what did you see being used? We moved us not them, we stepped into empty space, we rotated into empty space to avoid the line of attack. Every principle was used to avoid the attack and to do so in a manner that the strength, size and power of the Aggressor were not a factor.

The last drill gave us the first piece of Tactic One – Avoid the attack. Now that we have the needed movement we will build on that to an effective interception structure.

## ADD Intercept the Attack – Piece 2 of Tactic 1

## TOOL: The Cross Block Intercept (CBI)

The **structure**, the framing used to intercept the incoming assault has been called many things. In my Base system, Uechi Ryu Karate Jutsu, it is called a Cross Block and is a small piece of the main movement in the system called the Wauke, or Two-handed Circle Block. In some systems, this position is called Sword and Shield. We are going to add to the term Block here to reaffirm our intent: The Cross Block Intercept (CBI):

- The CBI is done with a rotation of the body **not** a movement of the arms.
- **The arms are MOVED, not moving**.
- The front arm (Arm closest to the Aggressor) remains high and is angled across, outside of the forearm turned outward.
- The rear arm (Arm farthest from the Aggressor) is angled downward and across, outside of the forearm turned outward.
- The two arms form an intercepting cross of bone (they do not need to touch each other, but the closer they are the better the shielding effect.).

As you train you will move from an Aggressor using a large attack to smaller and smaller attacks. Just as the Aggressor's attacks shrink so will the size of the CBI you use in response. The following descriptions and pictures show how the CBI shrinks to match the attack.

**Full Sized CBI:** Learning Tool for attacks from one step away. It builds the foundation structure.

**Small CBI:** Begins the shrinking of the CBI to match the Aggressor's closer attacks. Start to use this training attacks from an arm's reach away.

**Evolved CBI:** This is where we work to because it matches the shrinking of the aggressor's attacks from closer distances. But for learning you must build the base to have the evolved CBI work properly which is why we start training with the Large CBI.

**Survival Note:** With the CBI it is vital that the front arm (closest to the Aggressor) is angled upward and the rear arm (farthest from the Aggressor) is angled downward. This prevents a change of angle of the attacking knife from closing on your body. Reversing the arms will leave you open to a cut or stab. Only when circumstances prevent this should you use simply what works in the moment.

## Cross Block Intercept Drill for Large Movement Attacks

It is VITAL to recall that Intercepting the Attack is the SECOND piece of Tactic 1.

Piece ONE is and always will be AVOID THE ATTACK – MOVE YOU OFF THE LINE OF FORCE.

However, you will perform the CBI by placing your arms in position so that when you rotate at the finish of the step you will perform the CBI thus blending the two movements.

As a rule, whenever circumstance and situation allow you want to move so that you are on the outside of the weapon arm. This should be possible on four of the first five Basic Attacks, the Front Slash being the exception.

**TECHNIQUE: Thrusting Stab:**

- Once again both the Aggressor and Respondent are in a left foot forward stance for the descriptions below. (If you are the Respondent and working from a right foot forward stance when it says to do a sliding step you must step through.)

- With the knife in their right hand the Aggressor, from a distance of one large step, steps through and thrusts directly at their partner's midsection. (Note: you should repeat at different levels of thrust, but watch your eyes for safety.)
- The Respondent performs a Sliding Hip Rotation Step ending on the outside of the weapon arm.

Focus on stepping straight with your feet and allowing the hip rotation to pivot you on the ball of your left foot to move you off line ending with you perpendicular (at a "T") with the Aggressor. (Outside the weapon arm.)

As you are moving (Slide Step Hip Rotation) and rotating your hips and feet with your left arm high and right arm low perform the CBI.

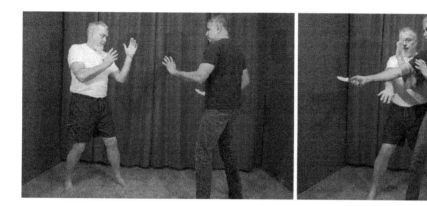

**NOTE THE PRINCIPLES:** Once again we moved us not them and we stepped into empty space. Both these principles mean there is no resistance to our action. We again rotated but this time we brought our arms into a strong but flexible (tendon power) structure. The rotation moved them into a strategic position (our arms were moved by our body movement, not moving on their own.) We finished in a balanced and stable structure. We are also now aligned to the weapon arm and facing empty space not into the Aggressor's structure. Stacking or layering principles is using more than one at once. At first this sounds complex but it isn't. Here we have used seven principles simply by sliding forward and rotating properly. Not a complex movement but rich in principles. Watch for these principles in the next pictures.

**Teaching notes:**

To begin training I recommend that the respondent has their arms already in the CBI position and simply step. Starting with arms in the CBI position shows there is no need for an arm movement because the body movement does everything. After a few repetitions, they can begin to work on bringing the arms into the CBI position as they rotate.

The resulting movement should not require force to work and should not meet force head on.

**Survival Note:** You MUST remember the CBI comes **simultaneously at the finish** of the avoidance step. The CBI is done as you move and rotate the hips. If you don't then the tendency is for people to try move directly to the CBI WITHOUT getting off line or using the hip rotation to do the movement. That results in a clash of force on force using a mere ineffective arm movement rather than a total body movement as they get off line.

*One factor making this system of knife defence workable is the consistent response to an attack. The first step to avoid and intercept is the same in the next three attacks as for the Thrusting Stab.*

**TECHNIQUE: Back Slash**

**TECHNIQUE: Over Hand Slash/Stab**

**TECHNIQUE: Uppercut Stab/Slash**

## TECHNIQUE: Front Slash

Because the front slash comes from outside and across your body you cannot get to the outside of the weapon arm and must move and intercept on the inside. This is why it is the last of the five attacked worked on.

**The principles used remain the same**: you move into empty space not into the Aggressor, you rotate moving your arms into the CBI, not just moving your arms. You are now in structure facing empty space not into their structure and strength.

The movement changes from a Slide Step Hip Rotation to a Step Through Hip Rotation.

- With the knife in their right hand the Aggressor, from a distance on one large step, steps through with their right foot and slashes across their body from right to left at their partner's midsection. (Note: you should repeat at different levels of thrust, but watch your eyes for safety.)
- The Respondent performs a Step Through Hip Rotation (right foot steps through and ends with the rotation). If, as the Respondent, you are working with your right foot forward you will Slide Step and rotate.

Focus on stepping straight with your feet and **allowing the hip rotation** (to the left open side) to move you off the line of force ending with you perpendicular (at a "T") with the Aggressor's weapon arm. (Inside the weapon arm.)

As you are moving and rotating your hips with **your right arm high and left arm low** perform the CBI. (NOTE: Always on a CBI your rear arm is lower and your front arm higher.)

- You still step into empty space and rotate to face Empty Space.

**THINK BACK TO THE OCR**, this is a practical, tactical version of that response. You withdraw your body from the knife and protectively throw your arms out to protect the body = Avoid while intercepting the attack. Because we start with the structure bigger for training and learning it looks less natural but that will change.

With the CBI you've created a **structure**. You have you arms in a strategic position (elbows in front of the body) giving them strength by being able to take force into that structure. If the elbows are out they will flair under pressure and the structure will fail. They are also slightly bent and if kept **LOOSE** (not rag doll relaxed) they can absorb a lot of force into the elasticity of the shoulders. (**Tendon Power**.)

We will use a "full sized" CBI when working against large movement attacks and then allow it to adapt and shrink as the attacks shrink in size and distance.

While there are other intercepts, I have found the CBI to be extremely effective and it has what I have found to be the best options for manipulating the Aggressor. Before staying with what you are comfortable I recommend giving the CBI a chance.

We have now covered both pieces of the first Tactic: Avoid while intercepting the attack. Now we must distinguish between the two sets of Tactics Distancing tactics and Closing Tactics.

# Distancing Tactics:

## ADD Propel the Aggressor away from you

To move the Aggressor, particularly one larger than we are, will make use of superior body mechanics.

**BIG LONG LEVER:**

The arm is a lever for the body. When the arm is extended, it can be used to manipulate the Aggressor's structure.

If a person stands and extends an arm and another person stands perpendicular to the arm, grabs it and simply walks forward or backward, the other partner cannot stop them from moving the arm.

This is the principle we will be using to rip structure from the Aggressor and take control.

Try it by having a partner stand with their arm extended and you step through or pull back the arm as they try to resist. Try it from inside and outside the weapon arm.

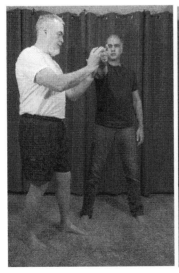

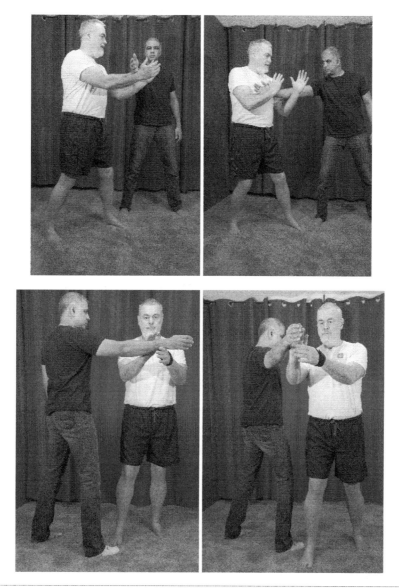

**SKILL NOTE:** The skill or knowledge you should take from this is that as long as you push the big long lever of their arm into the empty space at the side, they cannot stop you from moving their arm and therefore them.

## To Manipulate the Aggressor we use the principle of Shearing

Shearing is the principle required to make manipulating the Aggressor's structure and later clearing the weapon arm work properly.

Shearing is a cutting action.

Shearing is the cutting of one part of your body into and through a portion of the Aggressor's body.

This can accomplish many things:

- A shearing motion is hard to resist. Pressure applied directly, can be countered by a pressure placed in direct opposition. A shearing action is constantly shifting the angle at which you are applying pressure. This makes it much more difficult to counter.
- Shearing hits at an oblique angle and if that angle is correct (taking the Aggressor into empty space = not into their structure) it makes takedowns much easier.
- Shearing, when used to intercept a strike, means that you intercept the strike at ONE point on the Aggressor's limb, but you spread your contact all along your intercepting bone (forearm or shin). This means you can take a lot more impact without damage, while still inflicting damage on the Aggressor's limb.

You can shear through and over the triceps to disconnect (not dislocate) the Aggressor's shoulder from their back muscles to drive them over and down.

You can shear up into the Aggressor's shoulder joint (just off the back) to disconnect (not dislocate) the shoulder from their back muscles to drive them up onto one leg allowing you to step in and propel them away.

**NOTE THE PRINCIPLE:** Yes, we used the principle of shearing but as you can see from the pictures above and below we also use Empty Space. The arm shears through the Aggressor's arm but towards empty space – NOT into the Aggressor's structure and strength. Principles are meant to be layered/stacked to increase effectiveness. The more properly applied principles the more effective we are.

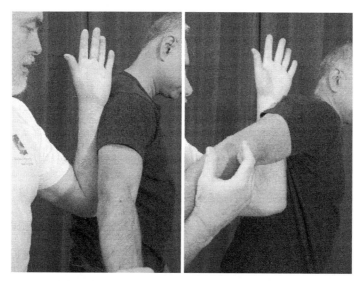

**NOTE THE PRINCIPLE:** We shear, we use empty space and when we move into the Aggressor to propel them away we do so Moving Our Centre, keeping our base underneath us, maintaining balance and structure.

The cutting angular action of a shear is vital to accomplish manipulating the Aggressor's structure, clearing the weapon arm, and maintaining control of that arm.

You also use the shear on the inside of the weapon arm to take control of the elbow.

The same action to shear the shoulder up so that you can propel the Aggressor away is used on the inside of the weapon arm. The shoulder is down and we need to shear it upward to disconnect it from the back.

**NOTE THE PRINCIPLES:** In the pictures above the elbow is taken into empty space, as is the shoulder in the pictures below.

Note (as pointed out in the picture below) the Aggressor's shoulder is down but by shearing we can raise it up to take their structure and balance.

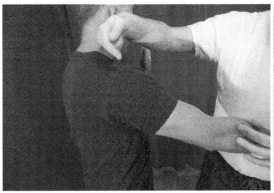 

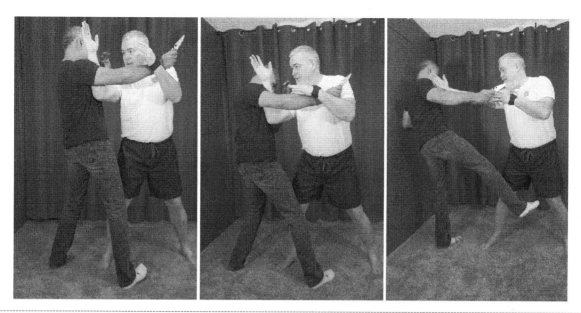

**Reality Note:** Yes, when you look at the pictures above the knife looks way too close to your neck for comfort but it isn't. A different view would show that the knife is not as close to the neck as you think and because you are launching the Aggressor the weapon arm flies outward and not towards your neck. Also, your rear hand is on the weapon arm and can hook at any time to prevent them slashing with the knife. Many might think "oh I would just cut your neck" but, when being knocked backwards on to their behinds they never actually do it.

Take a moment to look back over the pictures depicting shearing and look how we use empty space to enhance the effectiveness.

# DRILL: Shearing the Big Long Lever

**Purpose:** To experience how shearing through the arm increase the ease and effectiveness of manipulating the body with the arm as a lever. Look for the principles.

**IMPORTANT:** To enhance the effect of shearing we will be making use of **Empty Space**. Look for it.

**Part 1**

1. Stand so that you are perpendicular (at 90 degrees) to the weapon arm (where you would end up on the **outside** of the Aggressor's arm).
2. Place your right hand on the inside of the Aggressor's weapon forearm.
3. Place your left forearm on the outside of the Aggressor's weapon arm at the shoulder joint just off their torso.
4. Simply step straight forward into the empty space and AS YOU STEP use the outside edge of your left forearm to **CUT** through and up into the Aggressor's shoulder.

DO NOT think of moving the arm – simply think of stepping through it.

5.   Repeat and let the Aggressor try to hold themselves in position.

## Part 2

1.   Stand so that you are perpendicular (at 90 degrees) to the weapon arm (where you would end up on the in**side** of the Aggressor's arm).

2.   Place your left hand on the outside of the Aggressor's weapon forearm.

3.   Place your right forearm on the inside of the Aggressor's weapon arm at the shoulder joint just off their torso.

4.   Simply step straight forward into the empty space and AS YOU STEP use the outside edge of your right forearm to **CUT** through and up into the Aggressor's shoulder.

     DO NOT think of moving the arm – simply think of stepping through it.

5.   Repeat and let the Aggressor try to hold themselves in position.

# Apply Distancing Tactics

### Add: Propel the Aggressor Away

We need to regain **control of the distance**. The Aggressor has the control and closed on us with an attack but we want to either escape or have a chance to get to a weapon to protect ourselves. To do that we need to control the distance by making space.

### Technique: Thrusting Stab

- Just as previously the Aggressor has stepped in and extended their weapon arm forward to stab you.
- The Aggressor's power line is that direct line of the stab.
- The Aggressor's weapon arm is extended.
- Your movement and **rotation** have placed you perpendicular to the Aggressor's weapon arm.
- There are two full power lines: Arms 90 degrees to your body and arms out 180 degrees.
- Your arms are 90 degrees from your body facing to the Aggressor's arm and body.
- Your rotation moved you off their power line.
- Your rotation moved you so they are in your powerline.
- By rotating you are facing empty space.

This next part will emphasise why we move as we do.

1. Move your arms to the control points of under the shoulder joint and elbow.
2. Do all of the following together to slide and push, propelling the Aggressor away from you:

- Push on a slightly upwards angle.
- Slide step forward as you push.
- Shear upwards into the shoulder/arm to begin to break the structure of the Aggressor. (Do not try shearing into the back.)
- For added power, engage your mind by visualizing a line going from your arms up through their shoulders.
- Drive off your back foot press forward, move with your centre to propel the Aggressor away.

By shearing the shoulder up, you effectively disconnect it from the power source of the back, making it extremely difficult for them to resist being moved. You want to disconnect (not dislocate) the shoulder from the back.

**Survival Note:** DO NOT push into their body. Simply push on your power line up into empty space.

**NOTE THE PRINCIPLES:** Again, principles are not used in isolation, they are layered/stacked. Want to shear, do it into empty space. Want to shear and propel, do it into empty space and move with your centre = structure and balance. Look for each of these principles in the techniques.

### Stop the Threat: Deploy Weapon (or Grab an Improvised Weapon)

If your intent is to grab an improvised weapon, make sure you have already identified what it is and where and how to grab it quickly.

- The Aggressor has been propelled away from you.
- Step back (put distance between you and the Aggressor) and deploy a weapon (application dealt with later on).
- Place an object between you and the Aggressor for greater safety.

### Stop the Threat: Escape

- Run to a safer location.
- Place distance and objects between you and the Aggressor.
- Call for back up or law enforcement.

Now that you have responded to a Thrusting Stab with propelling the Aggressor away, work this response for the Back Slash, Over Hand Slash/Stab and Uppercut Stab/Slash.

### TECHNIQUE: Front Slash

The shear also works on the inside of the weapon arm just as it did on the outside.

We can shear to drive the Aggressor down which will be shown in a moment when we detail disable or control or (as shown before) you can shear the shoulder up so that you can propel.

Move your centre with a Step Through Hip Rotation.
- Just as before the Aggressor, from a distance on one large step, steps in and slashes across their body from right to left at their partner's midsection. (Note: you should repeat at different levels of thrust, but watch your eyes for safety.)
- The Respondent performs a Step Through Hip Rotation (right foot steps through). (Sliding Step for Respondents in a right foot forward stance.)

    Allow the **hip rotation** (to the left open side) to move you off the line of force ending with you facing empty space.

As you are moving and rotating your hips with **your right arm high and left arm low** perform the CBI. (NOTE: Always on a CBI your rear arm is lower and your front arm higher.)

**Propel the Aggressor Away**

Even though we are now inside the weapon arm we have still achieved all the points we wanted for this position.

1. Move your arms to the control points of under the shoulder joint and elbow.
2. Do all of the following together to slide and push, propelling the Aggressor away from you:
   - Push on a slightly upwards angle
   - Slide step forward as you push
   - Shear upwards into the shoulder/arm to begin to break the structure of the Aggressor.
- For added power, engage your mind by visualizing a line going from your arms up through their shoulders.
   - Driving off your back foot press forward to propel the Aggressor away.

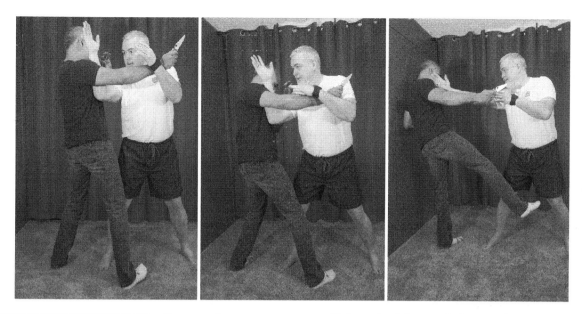

**NOTE THE PRINCIPLES:** Once again you can now see all the principles used above. The step to avoid the attack is into empty space, the rotation is also into empty space but also moves the arms into position. The arms are structured, the body balanced over its base. The shear is up into empty space and the propel is done by moving with the centre. BUT also look at the last picture. Under balance in the lists of principles it was noted to knock a person down you need to take their balance. By shearing up and through into empty space we "lifted" the Aggressor up onto one leg. This basically makes him a ball on a stick and his balance is YOURS. He is easy to knock over now. Your balance is kept and never given away, but their balance is for you to take, that is when you step into them.

Once you have propelled the Aggressor away you can continue to either escape or deploy a weapon.

## Closing Tactics Set

1) **Avoid while intercepting the attack**
2) **Control Lunge Step and Take Control of the weapon arm**
3) **Stop the threat: Control or Disable**

The First Tactic does not change so we will not repeat the movement drills or adding in the Cross Block Intercept. We will add Control Lunged Step and take control of the weapon arm and show how it blends into Stop the threat, and the strategies for survival.

# Control Lunge Step and Take Control of the Weapon Arm

Think back to the Shearing Drill. Both principles will be very much applied here. In addition, we are going to add in using gravity to increase our power and effect on the Aggressor.

**Control Lunge Step**

The Control Lunge Step is your primary movement as you gain control of the weapon arm.

It is a forceful, deeper, Step Through Hip Rotation or Sliding Hip Rotation Step into empty space.

- Think of a sprinter pushing off from a starting line and DRIVE forward with a step a little longer and deeper than a normal step.
- You move in an elongated deep stance with both your feet driving in a forward direction.
- Keep the feet in a straight line to your objective.
- **HOWEVER,** as you step in that straight line, rotate your hips as you move and complete the step.
- Advanced version: As you rotate the back foot will catch up bringing you back into your normal stance; however, keep your knees bent so that as the rear foot moves up you do not stand up taller thus taking the downward pressure off the weapon arm.

Step Through Hip Rotation Done as a Controlled Lunge Step:

Sliding Hip Rotation Done as a Controlled Lunge Step:

**NOTE THE PRINCIPLES:** Let's look at the principles used in performing a Control Lunge Step. First, the movement forward is done with your centre which keeps your structure. Second, you stay over your base to maintain balance, and third, the change in levels means you have sunk onto your centre = used gravity to add mass into a drop. You can always add mass to an action by dropping your centre BUT you want to do it without losing balance or structure.

**Skill Notes:**

The purpose of the Control Lunge step is not only that it is a powerful movement but also the lengthening of your base drops your centre. Dropping your centre uses gravity to manipulate the arm and destroy the Aggressor's structure.

In the advanced version allowing the rear foot to catch up to the elongated stance adds a last "jolt" of your centre moving forward. To see this jolt step into an elongated stance and note where your centre is, then shift the rear foot up so you are in a normal stance (the length of a normal step) and note again where your centre is now. See how far catching the rear foot up has moved your centre.

The long step drops your centre taking their balance, the last jolt of your centre coming forward is similar to the effect of an impact drill and adds to the destruction of their structure.

We know we can easily move that big long lever and now we want to own it!

## ADD: Control the Weapon Arm

Taking control of the weapon arm serves **two vital functions:** First, if we have a hold of the weapon arm we know where the knife is (where we are attached to the weapon arm acts as our sensors) and have a greater chance of sensing the attempts to kill us, and second, the purpose is to control and manipulate the Aggressor's structure by using the arm as a lever.

**Survival Note:** If you take control of the weapon arm in the manner we will describe, their structure will be broken, making the next step more efficient and effective.

We want to destroy the Aggressor's structure to the point they are in our control and one method is to place them in the position shown in the picture below.

Here is the how we accomplish that:

**CONTROL POINT**

The next piece of the puzzle to control the weapon arm is command over the Control Point.

The Control Point we need is **just above and behind the elbow**. (This was touched on in the Shearing Drill.) We will use the Control Point to manipulate the Aggressor by disrupting and destroying their structure.

One of your two arms (hands) will take this point as YOU move in to control the weapon arm. Most often it will be the front hand controlling the elbow unless we reverse directions, covered later.

As preciously shown in the first tactic "Avoid while intercepting the attack", taking control of the weapon arm begins by successfully avoiding the attack while intercepting with the CBI and places you in the position shown below. We need to move from there into the control position.

To demonstrate I will separate the actions of the front and rear hand.

It is important that as you step you MOVE TO the rear hand as it comes up into a bent elbow position. **Do not bring their arm to you, step to their arm.** The reason is because stepping TO the arm begins to take the Aggressor's structure. To demonstrate just try both bringing their arm to your body and stepping to their arm – observe the effect each has on the Aggressor.

**PRINCIPLE USED = MOVE YOU NOT THEM.**

The rear hand pins the weapon arm to your body using the top of the wrist bone. DO NOT hold the weapon arm with your hand – pin it with the wrist bone. Make their bones part of your skeletal structure so that when you move they are moved.

**PRINCIPLE USED = BONE SLAVING (MAKING THEIR BONES/SKELETON PART OF YOURS).**

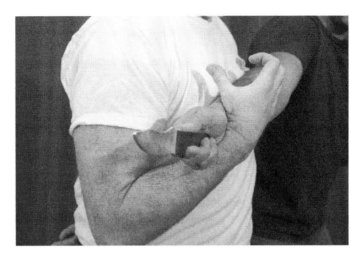

The Fronthad will make use of the Elbow Control Point as it shears through the arm.

**PRINCIPLES USED = SHEARING AND EMPTY SPACE.**

Step through moving to your rear arm pinning the weapon arm as the front arm shears through and over the control point. This will drive the shoulder over and down disconnecting it from the back muscles making the move effortless. It is important to note that by rotating as you step in you can then step through into empty space rather than trying to step into and press through their body.

As we move to the weapon arm and begin the shear you want to think of that amoeba enveloping and swallowing its food. By the time we are done the arm is pinned to our body and we smother it to us – think of taking all the air between that arm and your body out (in the pictures below right arm), our left arm has sheared over and we have stepped to the arm bracing it to our hip as we rotate.

**PRINCIPLES USED = SHEARING, MOVING WITH YOUR CENTRE, EMPTY SPACE PLUS SWALLOWING AND SMOTHERING.**

Our actions are causing a counter rotation in the weapon arm: If you have ever wrung the water out of a towel you will understand the principle of wringing. You grab each end twisting them in opposite directions to tighten the towel on itself. It affects the body dramatically. As we step to the weapon arm our rear hand moves up to pin it. By moving up it has a rotating or twisting upward effect. As we step we shear forward through and over the weapon arm having a rotating or twisting effect downward. The two opposite twists create the wringing action emphasized in the second picture below.

**PRINCIPLE USED = WRINGING (CREATING A COUNTER ROTATION SPIRAL).**

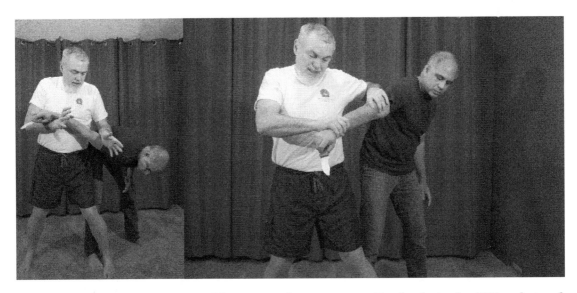

The Controlled lunge step is used to add power to the movement. You begin in the CBI and step deeply through and JUST AS YOUR FRONT FOOT HITS THE GROUND you rotate to your open side driving the Aggressor down and into the ground.

**PRINCIPLES USED = ALL THE PRINCIPLES WE'VE MENTIONED IN THIS SECTION ARE STILL THERE BUT I WANT YOU TO SEE THAT BY STEPPING INTO EMPTY SPACE YOU ALSO "MOVE YOU NOT THEM." HERE THAT ALSO MEANS AFFECTING THEIR STRUCTURE.**

**PRINCIPLE USED = NOTE THE EFFECT ON THE AGGRESSOR OF THE ROTATION PICTURED ABOVE.**

Once you intercept you may find the Aggressor attempting to get free just before you step. (We will deal later in the book with how to handle if they succeed in getting free and retracting the strike.) However, if you feel them pulling back DO NOT fight the pull. Resisting the pull is force on force and they have a high chance of succeeding. Instead think of being a ball on the end of an elastic band, as they pull you allow yourself to be pulled (move with the pull) and forcefully move in to shear and take control.

**PRINCIPLE USED = ELASTICITY**

**TECHNIQUES: Begin with the Thrusting Stab, then work the Back Slash, Over Hand Slash/Stab and Uppercut Stab/Slash:**

The following descriptions have both the Aggressor and Respondent in a left stance. If you are the respondent and normally stand in a right foot forward stance then do so; however, your first movement will be a Step Through Hip Rotation and not a Slide Step Hip Rotation.

LOOK for all the principles talked about so far.

**IMPORTANT:** For training, you must work each of the above four attacks separately with your partner knowing which one you are training.

- The Aggressor, from a distance on one large step through and attacks with one of the above four lines of force.
- The Respondent performs a Slide Step Hip Rotation to avoid and intercept with the CBI.
- You want to facing empty space.
- CBI: left arm high and right arm low.

- With a Step Through Hip Rotation step straight forward into the empty space and **Take Control of the Weapon Arm.**
- Your left (front) forearm is above their elbow. As you step through shear forward with the outside edge of your forearm through the weapon arm's triceps. This movement drives them forward and down disconnecting the shoulder with the back. (Down for control as opposed to up to propel.)
- As they are moved, continue to shear your forearm over and move you to the weapon arm.
- Allow the step to move you to rear (right) arm. As you step allow your right elbow to bend bringing the arm up thumb to chest hand perpendicular to the chest. Your wrist bone will come to contact with the weapon arm. Thinking of squeezing bone to bone squeeze all the air and space out from between your wrist and the weapon arm.
- With the Controlled Lunge Step, you will be dropping your centre slightly sinking onto the weapon arm and end the control lunge step with a rotation.
- ROTATE at the end of the Controlled Lunge Step.

**Skill Note:** It is important you finish with the HIP ROTATION.

As the Aggressor attacks (here a thrusting stab) we slide step and rotate intercepting with the CBI:

Using the CBI we take a step through with a Controlled Lunge Step to break their structure and take control of the weapon arm:

## ADD: Stop the threat: Control or Disable

Picture where we are at in our actions:

**Stop the Threat: Disable**

**Break the Arm:** The end position of taking control of the weapon arm places you in a perfect position to rotate with the front hand on the elbow and the rear hand on the weapon arm's forearm. A quick sudden rotation driving through the back of the elbow while drawing back on the rear arm can snap the limb disabling that weapon arm from doing more damage (in most cases).

**Strikes:** The positioning of the Aggressor allows for rear knee strikes to the head.

**Use the Ground:** Once you have their structure broken you can drop driving them into the ground. Using the ground as an impact weapon.

## Stop the Threat: Control

Again, I do not recommend going for control unless you have a duty or personal reason to do so as it is the riskiest option for your survival.

If you have a locking or control system you use or are required to use due to departmental policy, the position you have placed the Aggressor should allow for them to be enacted.

1. If not, stretch the Aggressor out onto their stomach by either stepping forward into and through their weapon arm or rotating through the weapon arm.

   Often it is easier to stretch them out by stepping with control of the weapon arm off on a 45-degree angle into **Empty Space** which prevents them from moving their base to follow.

2. Once stretched out, maintain control of the weapon arm and pivot so that you can drop your right knee onto the Aggressor's head pinning it to the ground.

3. Keeping the weapon arm up, extended, and against your chest, drop down with your other knee onto the torso of the Aggressor.

   OR shift your left knee onto the Aggressor's back, in the middle of the back almost to where the shoulder blades end. Move so your weight presses directly down on this point while maintaining control of the weapon arm.

4. In either case, the knee on the head or the back control point holds the Aggressor in position and requires you placing yourself over that point to keep control.

The other knee blocks the Aggressor from rolling.

5. From here the Aggressor can be kept in the pin until police arrive or you can proceed with your handcuffing techniques.

The Aggressor attacks with a Back Slash and we slide step in rotating to intercept with the CBI:

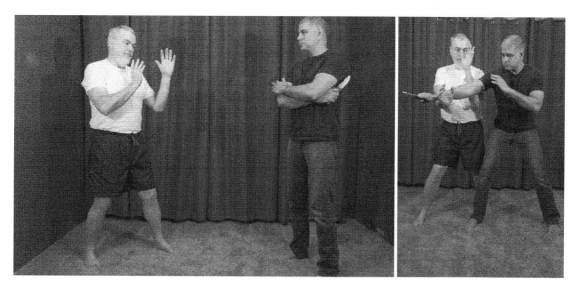

Using the CBI we step through to break their structure and rotate to drive them to the ground:

We step back bending our knees to drop our centre and mass on to the weapon arm to stretch the Aggressor out elongating him and bringing him to the ground:

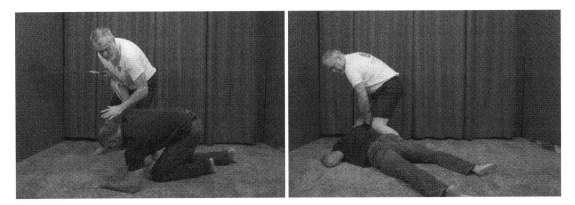

We now can use our knee on the centre point of the Aggressor's back to pin their body to the ground or shift to the knee on head position:

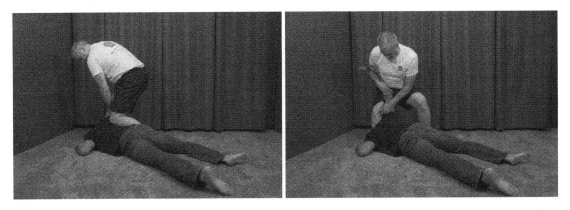

**NOTE THE PRINCIPLE:** You can now see the principles and how we have used them so far in the above pictures. Now, note what is used to take the Aggressor from their position of being on an elbow and two knees to flat on their stomach. The Aggressor has three points of contact on the ground; therefore, empty space is in the direction without contact. We step into that direction. Our left forearm is on their shoulder; therefore, we can rotate our arm using a shear to help move them into that hole. We can bend our knees as we move dropping our centre using gravity to sink our mass onto a point just off the shoulder joint. In addition, if you look there is another rotation into the shoulder as we draw them out is used. Why do we draw them out, stretch them? Remember that their base is those three points of contact, and by drawing them out off that base we take away their structure and their balance making it easier to "knock them down" flat on their stomach. We also use gravity to make the pin work.

## TECHNIQUE: Front Slash

- The Aggressor, from a distance on one large step, steps in and attacks with a Front Slash
- The Respondent performs a Step Through Hip Rotation to avoid and intercept the attack with a CBI (right arm high and left arm low.)
- You must be facing empty space, not into the Aggressor's structure.
- Your forearm impacts below the elbow (to prevent the arm from folding and bringing the knife towards you) and will then slide up to the elbow joint. Step through their arm shearing forward with your forearm.
- As they are moved, shear your forearm through the Control Point and move you to the weapon arm.

Alternate: As you step drive your right elbow up under their chin or into their head to drive them backwards.

- Allow the step to move you to the weapon arm as you bring your rear arm up thumb to chest hand perpendicular to the chest. Your wrist bone will come to contact with the weapon arm. Thinking of squeezing bone to bone squeeze all the air and space out from between your wrist and the weapon arm (wring out the towel).
- With the Controlled Lunge Step, you will be dropping your centre slightly sink onto the weapon arm and end the control lunge step with a rotation.

It is important as you step to shear through the elbow to take it with you as you step moving it out and away from the Aggressor's body.

Note the distance that is gained between the Aggressor's elbow and body.

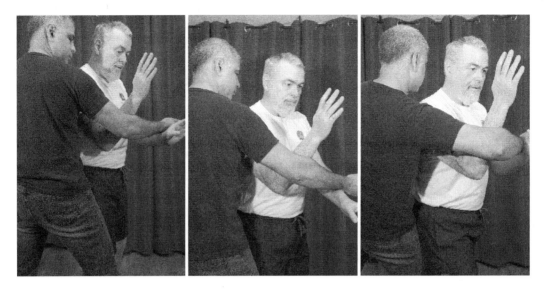

Using a Controlled Lunge Step will take you deep and ending with a rotation and sinking on the Aggressor's elbow will drop them to the ground allowing you to move into a control position that can be converted to a cuffing position.

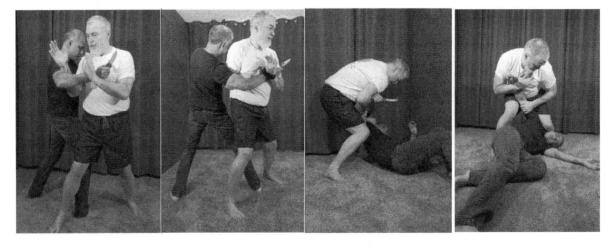

An alternative take down is to lock on with the Clamp (explained later), rotate to move the elbow away from the body, step back and rotate for the takedown.

In the second picture above note the distance of their elbow from their body achieved just before the takedown.

**NOTE THE PRINCIPLES:** In both methods above of taking the Aggressor to the ground the same principles are used even though they look like different things. A body rotation is used to move YOUR arms taking THEIR elbow to empty space (Bone Slaving). This moves their elbow out of structure (Remember we want our elbows in front of us). Once the elbow is off their base we use gravity to sink onto it. There is nothing below their elbow now because we have moved it off their base. Only empty space is below their elbow and we are about to use gravity and drop (sink) all our mass onto the elbow to put them on the ground. A final rotation to add power only makes it sweeter. In applying the Clamp note the second picture (above), the step back is done with your centre and because it is a longer step back our centre also drops; therefore, we add gravity to enhance the power of that step back.

**End the Threat - Disable:**

**Strikes:**  Once we close with the CBI, but before the takedown, we can control the weapon arm with the rear hand and deliver elbow strikes.

**Use the Ground:**  We can take control of the weapon arm and take them down driving them forcefully into the ground

**Break the Arm:** If we have taken them to the ground they are in a position for us to break the arm.

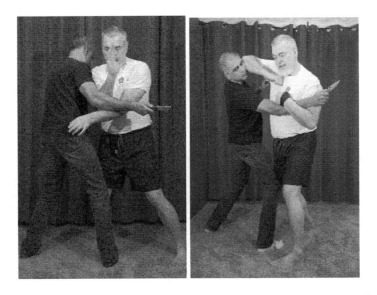

**Control:**

- They are off balance bent over backwards. We can continue the control taking them to the ground into a Side Control Position.

# Side Control Position:

In the side control position, you pull up on the weapon arm to slide your knees down pressing their head to the ground (think of the firemen of old sliding down the pole).

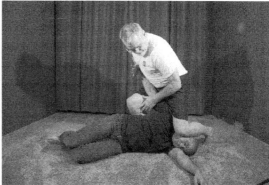

You want to make sure the neck is not level but is bent to disconnect (not dislocate) from the back – use the knee to hold it in that place:

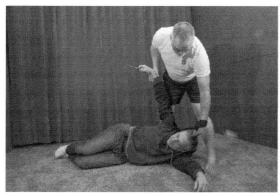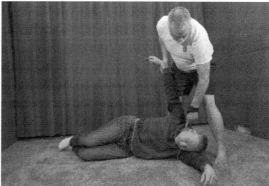

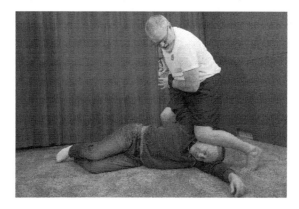

You want to make sure that their shoulder is pressed passed the midpoint or they can easily pull their bottom shoulder out to continue resisting:

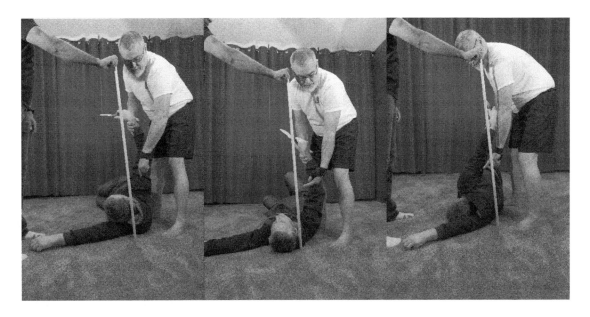

You want to think of their arm like a pole being driven into the ground:

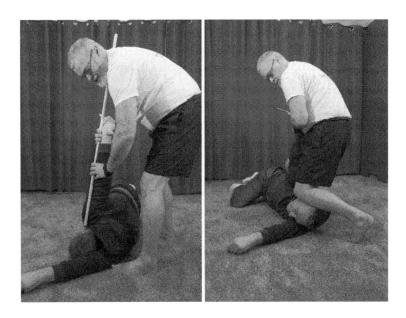

# Changing from Side Control to Face Down For Cuffing

## Technique One, The Lever Flip

With your right hand rotate the weapon arm so their elbow pit is pointed away from you and the elbow is across your knee or thigh.

Using the weapon arm as a lever and their elbow on your knee as the fulcrum turn to your right pulling down on their arm using the elbow fulcrum to pry them up off the ground (REMEMBER TO REMOVE YOUR KNEE FROM THEIR HEAD) rotate to your right and continue to pry with their arm turning and flipping them over onto their belly.

As they flip you can move your left hand to the back of their elbow to continue to have that control point covered.

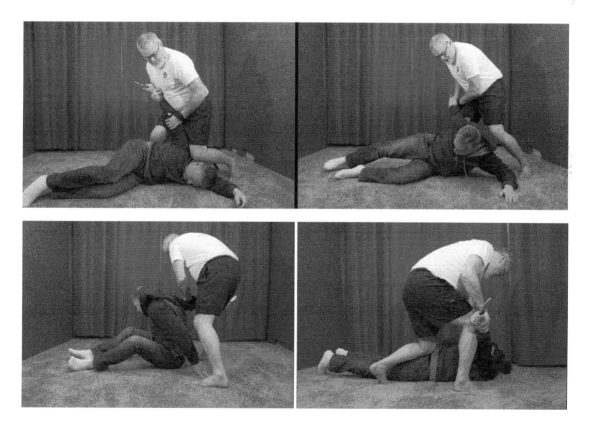

**NOTE THE PRINCIPLES:** Clearly, we are using leverage to pry them up by using their own arm as the lever and their elbow on our thigh as the fulcrum, but we are also prying the Aggressor up and into empty space and then using gravity to pressure the arm as we ROTATE them around.

## Technique Two, Knee Drive Roll Over

This can be harder to accomplish but when space prevents the flip from being used then this will do.

Drive your right knee into the back of their shoulder forcing them to roll forward.

Continue to press with your knee into their back as they roll.

Watch for their other arm to "pop" out, when it does grab it with your left hand and swing it out and behind them.

You will end with your knee in their back and both arms pulled back and controlled.

**NOTE THE PRINCIPLES:** We use gravity to sink our knee dropping our mass, but we also drive their shoulder towards empty space. WE DO NOT try to drive it through their structure.

## When Crap Happens – Reversal Alternatives

### From Outside the Weapon Arm – The Elbow Curl

We would all love that everything works out as we planned, but (shock and surprise) that doesn't always happen.

When crap happens in controlling the weapon you have some options. As we will see, you can clear the arm, you can control and step a different direction, or you can use this alternative move.

## Alternative Control and Technique

You are 90 degrees to the arm, you've begun to shear the weapon arm, but control isn't going as planned.

You can reverse the direction of the takedown.

1. Rotate your hips to the left and as you do fold your rear arm so it impacts the weapon arm's elbow bending it and moving it up, out away from their body, and off their base. (Raise your rear arm elbow as you rotate to do this.)
2. You will now do a bicep curl, just as you would curl a dumbbell, only as you curl your arm you also rotate it so your palm faces you.
3. Take a controlled lunge step backwards with the weapon arm pinned to your body and allow yourself to sink on the elbow.
4. Rotate again at the end of the step.
5. They will hit the ground.
6. Watch out for their heads as they collapse, inadvertent head butt.

We have intercepted an assault with the CBI but we either are not getting the control we want (the Aggressor got their balance back quickly) or we didn't rotate far enough and are facing into their structure and now in a struggle). We quickly rotate to get out of that spot and move their elbow out away from their structure.

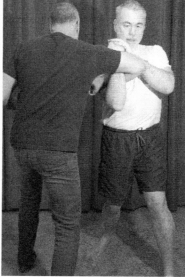

Now that we have moved their elbow out from their body we can Bone Slave it to us and step back with a rear sliding Control Lunge Step to rip the Aggressor off their base and then rotate again dropping our mass (using Gravity) onto their elbow driving them to the ground where we can move into side control position.

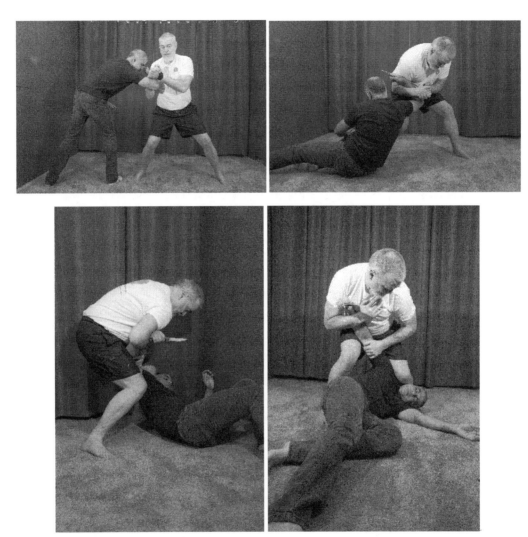

**NOTE THE PRINCIPLES:** We immediately use Bone Slaving to make the Aggressor's weapon arm part of our structure. We rotate to move through empty space taking the Aggressor's elbow off their base. You will note this is NOT an arm movement but the arms are moved by our body rotation. We then move our centre back dropping it using gravity to place our mass on the elbow as we step further pulling the aggressor's elbow off base, then we rotate and use gravity to drop on the elbow driving the Aggressor to the ground.

### From Inside the Weapon Arm – Elbow Roll

### Alternative Control and Technique

You are 90 degrees to the arm but control isn't going as planned.

You can reverse the direction of the takedown.

**Note:** The weapon in their right weapon hand, you are inside the weapon arm, your right foot is in front, and you will be rotating to your right to perform the move.

**VITAL:** You will be using the inside edge of your left forearm at the wrist joint to roll over top of the elbow without losing contact.

1. One of the ways to get the movement correct is to place the thumb side edge of your forearm (at the wrist) on the control point (above the elbow) with your thumb UP, then, as you rotate your body to the right, roll the edge of your forearm over the control point so that you keep contact and go until you are in the thumb DOWN position. This is a learning tool and I recommend losing it as soon as possible as an extended thumb can be grabbed.  We call this the Caesar Move.  Think of Caesar giving the thumbs down decision in the gladiator arena.

   **AS YOU ROLL YOUR ARM ALSO** hip rotate to your right allowing your rear (let hand) to roll the elbow over as you rotate.

   **NOTE:** Your arm should end on the back of their elbow – the Control Point.

2. Take a controlled lunge step backwards with the weapon arm ending either in a straight arm-bar or a figure four (Kimura) lock.
3. Rotate again at the end of the step.
4. They will hit the ground.

We have intercepted on the inside the weapon arm. We either need to change direction or we haven't rotated enough and are still facing their structure where we would have to fight force on force and strength on strength to get control. We rotate using The Caesar Move that allows us to break the Aggressor's structure without fighting their strength.

Now that we have broken their structure we can use a rear sliding control lunge step to stretch them out and elongate them further off their base. We can use our mass and gravity on the weapon arm to drive them into the ground and finish in control.

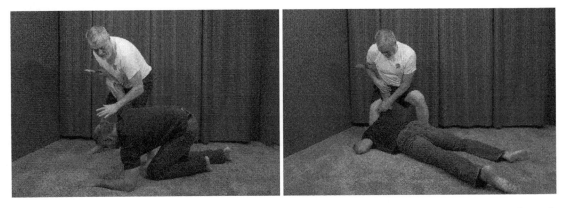

It is important to note that we are not trying to push the Aggressor's arm over or use strength to do this move. By using the inside of the wrist and rotating turning your arm from thumbs up to thumbs down the person is rolled over with little effort.

**NOTE THE PRINCIPLES:** I love this one. I love it more because far too often I see big strong guys trying to teach people to muscle a bigger person's arm over. Not going to happen. That roll of our wrist bone is a shear. The rotation MOVES our arms as the wrist bone rolls. If you look the rotation applies the force into empty space and NOT into the Aggressor's structure. The take down uses the arm as a lever and stepping back with our centre adds gravity. The step back also stretches the aggressor out into empty space and off their base.

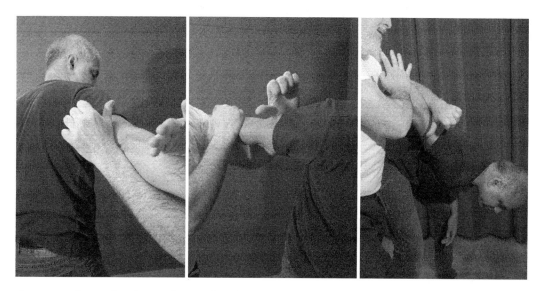

**In the pictures above look at where the thumb is pointing – always to empty space...**

**Note:** The action of your wrist against the weapon arm as you rotate turning the thumb from up to down is very similar to the tool used to cut copper pipe. If you have ever cut pipe the tool is tightened until the cutting edge is against the pipe then the tool is rotated around the pipe. This action is no different you are using your cutting tool (your wrist bone) to cut into and around the pipe (the weapon arm.)

- In the next two drills look for the principles just described being used.

## Drill: Elbow Manipulation

We are going to isolate the skill of manipulating the elbow (see "Addendum #2: Micro Moment Skill Set Progressive Training" for details on this approach.)

**Part 1**

1. Get in position on the outside of the weapon arm and then rotate left and curl taking control of their arm then step back and rotate.
2. Unwind, let them up and repeat.
3. Repeat as your partner adds resistance.
4. Repeat again against the left arm.

## Part 2

1. Get in position on the outside on the weapon arm, rotate right taking control of the weapon arm, and then step back and rotate.
2. Unwind, let them up and repeat.
3. Repeat as your partner adds resistance.
4. Repeat again against the left arm.

**NOTE:** After a while, when you get the hang of it, you can rotate back and forth alternating the moves without letting them recover.

# Alternative Using "The Clamp"

## The Clamp

The Clamp is a Bone Slaving Tool.

The Clamp is an exceptionally useful tool that can be applied in many situations during the knife defence. The purpose is to immobilize the Aggressor's arm (usually the weapon arm) so that we can manipulate and destroy their structure. This is NOT a compression lock, you must think of it like a "clamp."

A clamp is a simple device. It has two arms that are pulled together usually by a spring to hold something in place.

For us, our hands are going to form the fulcrum. Our forearms are the arms of the clamp. Our muscles and tendons will act as the spring.

The grip to pin the fulcrum point together will be formed by one of two suggested grips:

- The Gamble Grip, or the Closed Full Hand Grip, is formed by placing your palms together and wrapping your fingers and thumb around the hands to grasp.
- The Gene Labell Grip, or the Open Three Finger Grip, is formed by placing your palms together BUT placing (for example) your right thumb between the index and middle finger of your left hand, and then wrapping the fingers and thumb around the hand to grasp.

The clasping part of the Clamp will be the edges of your forearms along the bones.

The Clamp can be applied to any part of the Aggressor's arm, but the forearm below the elbow allows great manipulation of the arm and Aggressor's body, although in some positions clamping onto the bicep gives you control over the shoulder for a takedown.

## Applying the Clamp

1. Grasp your palms in one of the two grips, apply the clamp to their forearm.
2. Begin to rotate towards your rear arm.
3. Allow your movement to catch up to the arm in the direction of your rotation (here your rear arm).
4. Begin to squeeze your forearms together.
5. **Roll your hands so the back of the hand in the direction you are rotating is facing up. Use a swooping motion with the front arm. (I.e. If you are rotating right the back of the right hand is up and the palm down.)** Adding a roll and spiral always makes things better.
6. Squeeze and force all space and air out from between your forearms and the Aggressor's arm. (Swallow and Smother.)
7. Think of clamping the bones of your forearms to the bones of the weapon arm.
8. Pull (compress/smother) your arms towards your chest, Bone Slaving their structure to yours with the Clamp.
9. Now they are trapped and you can continue to rotate with your body either direction separating their arm from their structure and then drop onto their arm driving them to the ground.

Clamp on forearm (Inside and Outside the weapon arm):

Clamp on Bicep/Triceps (Inside and Outside the weapon arm):

**Play with the Clamp.**

Take this and play with it.

Apply it on all parts of the Aggressor's arms. Work from outside and inside the weapon arm. Clamp onto the forearm and the bicep/triceps. Test rotating either directions. Testing taking the elbow off their base and sinking on it.

PLAY – Seriously take this tool and try it out every way you can and manipulate your partner as much as you can.

Once you start to get it have them increase resistance and continue to PLAY.

If your partner doesn't feel like you might be able to snap their forearm in the Clamp – keep working on that bone crushed to bone thought process.

Many find the clamp becomes a go-to technique and works particularly well on larger Aggressors. When I taught the Clamp at the 2017 Alberta Peace Officer's Annual Convention one female officer said that the previous methods of taking control of the weapon arm she had been taught involved grabbing onto the weapon arm bicep. She was smaller of stature and said her hand didn't fit around most men's bicep, so those methods of control did not work for her; however, The Clamp became her best friend and within a few attempts she was locking on and manipulating much bigger stronger fellow officers.

# Left Handed Aggressors

Before we move on and change the distance of the attack we need to address the issue and possibility of the attack being left handed. While not probable, there are changes to the approach that are not hard to adapt to because you have already made the adaption when shifting to the inside on a front slash. However, the different visual of a left handed assault needs to be conditioned until you are comfortable with.

Approximately 10% of the population is left handed. Only 1% change dominant hand depending on tasks and ambidexterity is even more rare. Going against a left-handed Aggressor is unlikely but still possible.

Therefore, 1 to 2 attacks out of 10 should be with the left hand when training.

HOWEVER, that will not be enough to be comfortable with the slight shifts in approach needed.

TO OVERCOME THIS

## DRILL: THE RIGHT HAND LEFT HAND

This drill should be placed after you complete each change in distance and every now and then to ensure you remain comfortable with protecting yourself from a left handed attack.

1. Pick an attack and start from the distance you have just learned. Therefore, the first time should be with a long step straight thrust.
2. Attack with the right hand.
3. Attack with the left hand.
4. Repeat, switching each attack until you have attacked 10, 20, or 30 times with each hand.
5. Hide the knife and your hands behind your back.
6. Attack with either hand.
    - If the Respondent handled it without hesitation go to the next attack and distance.
- If Respondent hesitated, then repeat until they do not.

One "side effect" you might notice is ending up on the inside of the weapon arm when you meant to end up on the outside, but do not panic. You already know what to do on the inside from the Front Slash techniques so in the end, while outside is preferable, it is not a failure.

**Teaching Note:** In the Right Left Right Left drill only the initial response is required because that is what you are trying to condition. You can go on and complete your strategy but that isn't always required, although completing the left side is a good idea as some are thrown by the shift in position.

**NOTE:** See "Addendum #1: Operant Conditioning to Habit Response" for a full explanation of why the next two drills are done as they are, for example in slow motion.

The methods used in this knife defence are not yet "part of what you do" and therefore you need to go slow to ensure you stay with using this method rather than reverting to a previous method.

You also go slow so you do not cover up flaws in performance with attributes such as speed or strength. These techniques done properly work when done slowly, because they use sound principles and body mechanics.

# DRILL: Operant Conditioning #1

- The partners stand one large step apart.
- The Aggressor partner has a knife hidden from view, and then **IN SLOW MOTION** pulls it and attacks with any of the main attacks: Thrusting Stab, Front slash, Back Slash, Over Hand Slash/Stab or Uppercut Stab/Slash.
- Out of every FIVE attacks have at least one has the knife in the left hand.
- Trade roles.

**Teaching Note:** The illustrations above just show the opening response but in the Operant Conditioning Drill you MUST take it the rest of the way to full completion of your strategy and survival.

# DRILL: Operant Conditioning #2

- The partners stand one large step apart.
- The Respondent closes their eyes.
- The Aggressor has a knife hidden from view, and then **IN SLOW MOTION** pulls it and attacks with any of the main attacks: Thrusting Stab, Front slash, Back Slash, Over Hand Slash/Stab or Uppercut Stab/Slash.

AT ABOUT HALF WAY INTO THE STEP THE AGGRESSOR WILL SAY BEGIN.

- **WHEN THE AGGRESSOR SAYS BEGIN THE RESPONDENT OPENS THEIR EYES AND ACTS.**
- Out of every FIVE attacks have at least one has the knife in the left hand.
- Trade roles.

**Teaching Notes:** Just as in the 1st Operant Conditioning Drill this illustration only shows the initial response and in practice your MUST take it the rest of the way to complete your strategy and survival.

When you do a move against another person all kinds of crap gets involved and, if it fails, often you are not doing either what you are supposed to do or what you think you are doing.

Removing the distraction, the partner, allows a third party to see if you are actually doing what you need to, if your execution is correct.

For example, a person I was teaching was struggling. When I had them do the move on their own, it was clear they stepped, landed, then rotated, when what they needed to do was step AND rotate AS their foot landed, NOT after their foot landed.

When entangled in the assault of a partner that vital distinction is hard to observe, but once the distraction of the partner was removed it was easy to see and therefore easy to correct.

Proper execution of form is the reason many martial art styles do patterns. So, if you or a student are struggling, separate them from their partner and see if what they are doing is what they are supposed to be.

Better to do ten repetitions with proper execution than a hundred incorrectly.

## DRILL: Left to Right to Left to Right CBI

Having the front hand up and the rear hand down is vital to the execution of the techniques that follow the intercept as well as a safer position to be in.

Some find switching hard to do so this drill both helps with that issue and introduces us to the movement that will be needed when the distance closes.

1. The Aggressor takes a training knife in each hand.
2. The Respondent stands in front of them inside arm's reach.
3. The Aggressor front slashes with their right hand.
4. The Respondent rotates left to intercept with the CBI (right hand high, left hand low.)

5. The armed partner front slashes with their left hand.

6. The Respondent partner rotates right to intercept with the CBI switching to left hand high, right hand low.

7. The Aggressor repeats right, left attacks over and over beginning SLOWLY and as the Respondent partner is successful switching for right hand high CBI to left hand high CBI the attacks speed up to the breaking point.

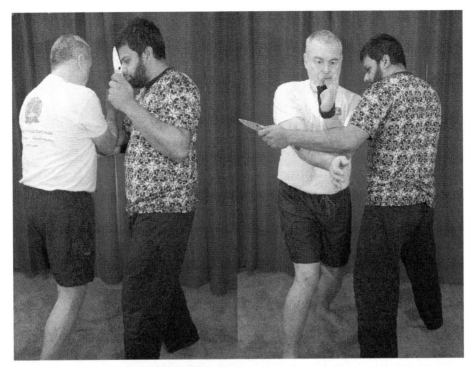

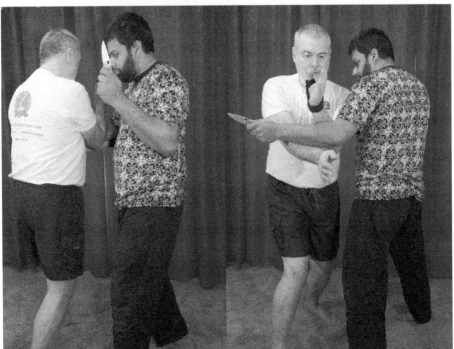

IT IS IMPERATIVE that you make sure the Respondent partner is rotating and not just moving their arms back and forth: the "T" position to the weapon arm must still be accomplished with each CBI.

# Preparing for Small Movement Attacks (Within an arm's reach)

The big movement attacks are good for training and you may even encounter them. Those in Law Enforcement may come on a scene with a person brandishing a knife, often due to a substance induced state or mental health issues.

However, more common will be the knife pulled from concealment and up close to the intended victim.

Distance = Time = Opportunity

The bad guys know this too, so they "shrink" their movement to reduce the distance, to reduce your time, to reduce your opportunity.

Just as the bad guy shrinks their movements **so must you**.

There will not be any stepping to engage, because they are already in engagement distance. The only movement you will have time to do is Rotation. Both your movement and the CBI will shrink.

The large full CBI will become a Small Cross Block Intercept, but it retains a similar form and function.

**The quickest movement is a body rotation, to turn about an axis or a centre**

Your centre is the axis you are going to rotate around and you are going to add that movement to the Tactical Sensitivity Drill's avoidance (Drill coming). This is the Hip Rotation from the movement section and just used in the Left to Right to Left to Right Drill.

It is vital you rotate around your centre NOT around one of your feet. The difference is the effect you will have on the Aggressor.

But first a drill.

Again, the following is a "drill." It is not intended to be real, it is intended to give you a deeper sense of how a knife will move and how you should move in response. One skill that rarely has a drill to teach it is reading the attack. This drill begins to work on that. I cannot tell you how often someone new to knife defence training will move INTO the path of the blade simply because they could not read where and how the knife was going to move. This drill's purpose is to teach that reading.

As unreal as this drill is, if in a real situation it provides you with "just" enough extra avoidance, then that would be a nice bonus to the skill sought in this drill.

In the moment of a sudden assault there is no time to think "Oh, should I move my body this way or this way not to die?"

The moment the blade is coming towards us we must "know" how we should be moving to avoid it. The only way to do this is to separate that "moment" out into a practice all its own. The purpose is to habituate which way to move through a tactile body training.

**NOTE:** I call this "Micro Moment Skill Set Progressive Training," which mean the segregating skill set you need at one point in a conflict and only for a micro moment. It is segregated and expanded so that it can be ingrained into your habitual use. See "Addendum #2: Micro Moment Skill Set Progressive Training" for complete details.

> **REALITY NOTE:** Once again this is a drill from which to learn. BUT the movement in this drill can often be very fine. While you learn, and it is fun, and you get the skills needed, for Law Enforcement and Security, once a protective vest and equipment is put on that "fine" movement will no longer be there due to the restrictions of the gear. However, more gross movements will be possible along the same lines, giving again more opportunity and that knowledge of how the blade attacks a body. I highly recommend repeating all drills and training in full gear.

# DRILL: Tactical Sensitivity

Reminder: a drill teaches a skill or principle; it is NOT a representation of how to fight back. And once vest or gear is added these movements alter to fit the changed Circumstance.

FOR ALL STEPS START SLOW AND BUILD SPEED AS YOUR PARTNER'S SKILL INCREASES.

AT EACH STEP DROP THE SPEED DOWN AND BEGIN THE PROGRESSION OF GETTING FASTER ALL OVER AGAIN.

> **TOOL REQUIRED:** You need a longer rigid training weapon, such as a wooden or metal trainer Bowie knife, or simply cut and sand a piece of doweling to about 12 inches.

**Part 1**

- Move and minimize. YOU CANNOT TOUCH THE ARMED PARTNER WITH HANDS ARMS LEGS, ANYTHING. NO GUIDING THE WEAPON ARM WITH ANYTHING OTHER THAN YOUR BODY.

- The Aggressor places the knife (tool) on the unarmed partner's body and begins to cut and/or stab attempting to have "continuous" contact with the blade on the body.

- The Respondent tries to read the cut or stab and move their body in a manner that either avoids the damage or minimizes it.

- Here your ability to remain loose and not allow tension into your body will be judged. It is exceptionally hard to read through tactical contact if you are tense. Remain **loose**. Loose (not ragdoll relaxed) enhances everything, tension detracts from everything.

**NOTE:** This is not always going to work well due to the continuous contact. You're not doing anything to interfere with the armed partner yet and it is just tough. Success at avoiding or minimizing the effect of the knife is only part of this drill. The purpose is to learn how the knife will move cutting or stabbing you from various angles. This isn't a contest.

## Part 2

- Move, minimize, and close.
- The Aggressor repeats their role of continuous contact and attack.
- The Respondent now not only tries to read the cut or stab and move their body in a manner that either avoids the damage or minimizes it, BUT they also try to slide/step in AS they move, to close with the armed partner.

**NOTE:** Due to the continuous contact you will find yourself in places where just getting out of them is all you accomplish, but attempt to close as often as possible.

## Part 3

- Move, minimize, and touch.
- The Aggressor repeats their role of continuous contact and attack.
- The Respondent now not only tries to read the cut or stab and move their body in a manner that either avoids the damage or minimizes it, BUT they also "touch" the weapon arm following where it goes WITHOUT GUIDING IT AT ALL (this is the difficult part).

What we want to gain here is the sticking of your hands to the weapon arm WITHOUT losing your movement.

**NOTE:** The hard part is not guiding the weapon arm BUT you must not do it. If you start to guide NOW, you will lose the body movement and it is the combination later on that brings the most success. Right now you want to learn to "feel" where the blade is going.

**NOTE THE PRINCIPLES:** The main principle I want you to note is that the arms are moved by the body rotation and not just moving. Making the movement or the arm and the movement of the body into ONE MOVE is vital.

## Part 4

- Move, minimize, and guide.
- The Aggressor repeats their role of continuous contact and attack.
- The Respondent now not only tries to read the cut or stab and move their body in a manner that either avoids the damage or minimizes it, BUT they also can use the armed partner's incoming force to guide them.

**NOTE:** Now that you can guide the weapon arm, the challenge you face is to do it in conjunction with your movement and with their force. DO NOT FIGHT THEIR FORCE. Do not close yet!

## Part 5

- Move, minimize, guide, and close to a strategic "hands on the weapon arm" position.
- The Aggressor repeats their role of continuous contact and attack.
- The Respondent now not only tries to read the cut or stab and move their body in a manner that either avoids the damage or minimizes it, BUT they also can use the Aggressor's incoming force to guide them AS they **close in** with hands on the weapon arm to control it. (Think CBI position and the Control Point at the back and above the elbow, and the rear hand smothering the weapon arm to your body.)

**Note:** The challenge is to have a real control of the weapon arm and the armed partner should "check" at the end of each movement to see that the unarmed partner does.

Step 6

Move, minimize, guide, and close to a strategic "hands on the weapon arm" position.

- This step is the same as step five, only now you use a shorter knife.

**NOTE THE PRINCIPLES:** This drill introduces sticking, adhering, guiding and leading rather than clashing and forcing the Aggressor to move the weapon arm in a different direction. Tim Cartmell says you must never alarm your opponent. When we clash, or try to force a movement on the Aggressor they know their movement has or may fail and they will change and do something else. That means we have a new attack to deal with. What we want to do is alter the course of the blade by encouraging the Aggressor to do more of what they are already doing. Think of being able to nudge a bowling ball just enough as it travels that by the time it reaches the end of the lane it is a gutter ball. The action is not enough to alarm the Aggressor but enough to alter what they are doing and by the time the Aggressor is alarmed it should be too late. The other skill worked at the end when you are too close and control is that each rotation should bring the weapon arm into your small CBI. Learning to lead them into the trap of the CBI is an important skill to have as the distance of the attack gets closer and closer. You want to learn to read the attack and not just with your eyes but with your contact to the Aggressor. This is another reason we want to attach to that weapon arm with the CBI. The Tactical Sensitivity Drill focuses on teaching how to read the attack but at the same time it introduces sticking and adhering to the weapon arm. It introduces guiding the weapon and eventually leading it into the CBI. All the principles work towards accomplishing our goal without alarming the Aggressor until it is too late for them. As unreal as this drill may seem (and it is not real knife defence) it is one of the most important drills because of what it teaches.

## Assaults from within an arm's reach

### Look for the principles used in our responses to the attacks.

Because we have lost distance we have lost time. Tactic One, avoid while intercepting the attack, is done without a step, only a rotation.

### What Changes?

The movement used by the Aggressor going from a longer distance away to this closer distance changes by SHRINKING.

- The Aggressor does not have to move as far.
- The stab shrinks from a long thrust.

Everything the Aggressor does shrinks as the distance shrinks.

THEREFORE, everything the Respondent does will shrink.

- You will not step and rotate.
- Your movement will shrink to just a rotation.
- The Full CBI will shrink to cut the time and to make the next steps easier.

The arm positions, front up and rear down, do not change.

The Full CBI was important to use on the long-distance attacks as a learning tool to have the right control position.

### The Small CBI

Arms are not fully extended and the V formed is tighter and smaller.

**TRAINING NOTE:** The attacks in the small movement section should come from a concealed position. Thrusting Stab: the knife is held out of sight behind the thigh. Front Slash: The Aggressor's arms are crossed with the knife out of sight, right arm under the left so the knife in the right hand can be hidden.

**NOTE:** Again, if you work from a right foot forward stance then you should also train from a right foot forward stance. Here we are using only a rotation and even from the right stance the rotation is still in the direction described – that will be even more important later. You will have to rotate a little farther than a Respondent in a left foot front stance but that can be accomplished by allowing your left foot to "travel" as you rotate so that you end still in a right stance. (Yes, this means you will be rotating to the close side, but so will the Respondent in a Right Stance for a left-handed Aggressor.)

## Distancing Tactics Set

**TECHNIQUES: Begin with the Thrusting Stab, then the Back Slash, Over Hand Slash/Stab and Uppercut Stab/Slash:**

Once again, this system keeps responses the same for the first four attacks, the avoid and intercept is the same and the follow up to either escape or deploy a weapon. Work each one separately with your partner knowing which one you are training.

- The Aggressor, from inside arm's distance, attacks with one of the first four attacks.
- The Respondent performs a quick Hip and foot Rotation to the right. (Ending outside the weapon arm.)
-  There is no step here because the attack is too close and too fast, you only have time to rotate your body and feet. Rotating not only your hips but also your feet ensures your whole body rotates.
- You moved your arms into the small CBI position AS you rotated so your left arm is high and right arm low. The small CBI is a quicker position to get into than the large CBI.
- We can now make use of weakening their structure by driving in and shearing up to raise their shoulder and drive towards "empty space" behind them and not into their structure to propel them away.

We rotate and intercept with the CBI:

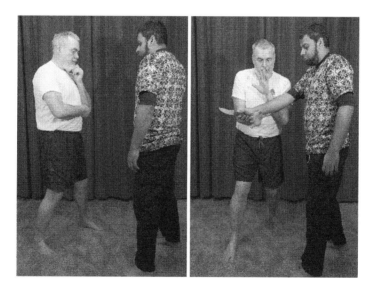

We move into the Aggressor and move to the weapon arm (do not try to bring the weapon arm to you) as we bend our rear arm up. Our front arm stays structured and moves up to the shoulder joint. Notice our this combined action rotates and takes the structure away from the Aggressor setting them up to be propelled.

Once the Aggressor has been propelled away continue to either escape or deploy a weapon.

**TECHNIQUE: Front Slash**

- The Aggressor, from inside arm's distance attacks with a front slash.
- We are going to use the same quick body and feet rotation as with the other attacks only this time to the left moving our arms into a small CBI with your right arm high and left low.
- We are again going to drive in and shear the shoulder up (this time on the inside of the shoulder joint) and continue to drive forward into the empty space behind the Aggressor.

We rotate and intercept with the CBI – note the front hand is below the elbow joint to prevent the Aggressor from bending the arm and cutting:

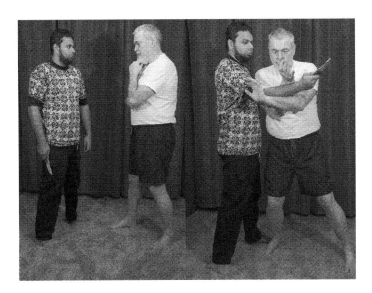

Again, we move to the Aggressor shearing and slamming our front arm up, through and into the shoulder joint as our rear arm bends to contact the weapon arm (attaching our sensor). The impact drives the Aggressor back quickly and flairs their arms out and away from their body (taking the knife away from our neck.)

Once the Aggressor has been propelled away continue to either escape or deploy a weapon.

## Closing Tactics Set

1) **Avoid while intercepting the attack**
2) **Control Lunge Step and Take Control of the weapon arm**
3) **Stop the threat: Control or Disable**

**TECHNIQUES: Begin with the Thrusting Stab, then the Back Slash, Over Hand Slash/Stab and Uppercut Stab/Slash:**

Again, you will train each attack separately.

- The Aggressor, from inside arm's distance, attacks with one of the four first attacks.
- Just as in Distancing Tactics Set we use the quick body and feet rotation AS we move our arms into the small CBI.
- In Training (not Practice = Operant Conditioning Drills) you can take a moment to ensure you have rotated so you are not only off the line of the attack but also no longer facing into their structure and strength.

- Because you are not facing their structure you can step with intent into empty space shearing their weapon arm (or applying the Clamp) to take control of it.
- You want to make sure all the principles are applied: moving to the weapon arm (not moving it to you), smothering the weapon arm to you by bringing the rear hand inside wrist edge to your body to add that wringing effect as you shear through the control point (above and behind the elbow) with the front arm.

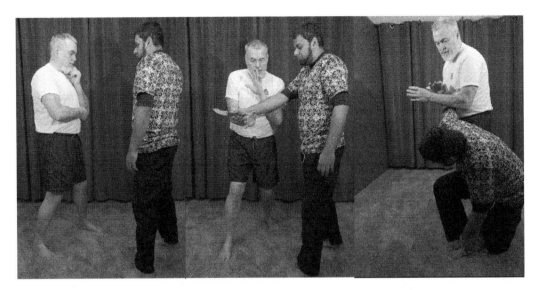

Once you have taken control of the weapon arm and disrupted their balance and structure you can end the threat by either breaking the arm and/or striking or continue to take them to the ground into a control position.

**NOTE:** The thrusting stab and the uppercut stab/slash when close can change angles, sometimes coming in on a curve, which makes it a front slash/stab and going inside the weapon arm is safer.

### TECHNIQUE: Front Slash

- The Aggressor, from inside arm's distance attacks with a front slash.
- Just as in Distancing Tactics Set we use the quick body and feet rotation, this time to the left applying the Small CBI right hand high left low.
- We are now inside the weapon arm rotated facing away from their structure and strength.
- The inside of the elbow is going to be our focus for taking control and stepping through that point into the empty space we are now facing to disrupt their balance and destroy their structure.
- Remember that you must move their elbow away from their body before you can complete disrupting and destroying their structure.

The picture below shows an alternative action using the Clamp.

You can continue to stop the threat by either disabling or by taking control.

**NOTE THE PRINCIPLES:** You will have seen that all the principles previously used and pointed out were still used. If you missed them reread the last attack section and the notes on the principles and look the above attacks over again. I'll point them out again in the next section but I want you to look for them here.

> **Teaching Note:** We have just completed the attacks from within arms reach and must now repeat The Left Hand Right Hand Drill to condition responding to the knife in either hand.

## DRILL: Operant Conditioning #3

We are going to repeat the Operant Conditioning drills from the closer distance attack.

- The partners stand within an arm's reach.
- The Aggressor will have a knife hidden from view and then **IN SLOW MOTION** pull it and attack with any of the main attacks: Thrusting Stab, Front slash, Back Slash, Over Hand Slash/Stab, or Uppercut Stab/Slash.
- Do one out of every FIVE attacks with the knife in the left hand.
- Trade roles.

## DRILL: Operant Conditioning #4

- The partners stand within an arm's reach.
- The Respondent closes their eyes.
- The Aggressor will have a knife hidden from view and then **IN SLOW MOTION** pull it and attack with any of the main attacks: Thrusting Stab, Front slash, Back Slash, Over Hand Slash/Stab. or Uppercut Stab/Slash.

JUST BEFORE THEY MOVE, THE AGGRESSOR WILL SAY BEGIN.

- **WHEN THE AGGRESSOR SAYS BEGIN THE RESPONDENT MAY OPEN THEIR EYES AND ACT.**
- Do one out of every FIVE attacks with the knife in the left hand.
- Trade roles.

# Preparing for Assaults from within One Foot

# DRILL: Hand

This drill is to give you the skill set of Very Small Movement Control.

Once again, this is not a full "go to" move but in the moment, it could be a life saver and it is a vital component of your response in the very close quarter attacks as you will see. (Another reminder that this is a DRILL and not REAL.)

The Aggressor is restricted in their movement for this drill. They must not pull the knife back and away. They must keep the knife out in front of them.

They must keep the knife within a restricted range of 45 degrees to the left and 45 degrees to the right. Other than that, they will try to slash and stab their partner.

The Respondent will connect to the weapon arm's hand with their wrists.

Using Hip Rotation and Wrist Rotation they will stick to the weapon arm and (in step two) guide it away from slashing or stabbing them.

Movement Restrictions:

Only out to 45 degrees to the Aggressor's right:

Only out to 45 degrees to the Aggressor's left:

They cannot pull their arm back to break contact:

The goal is to be as light on the weapon arm as possible and to guide rather than force the knife to miss.

## Part 1

- The Aggressor doesn't attempt to cut or stab their partner. Instead, they move the knife back and forth and in many directions.
- The Respondent keeps their hand or wrist on the weapon hand's wrist as lightly as possible, only moving with them and maintaining contact with NO attempt to manipulate the Aggressor's movements. Stick and adhere.
- The Respondent should use hip rotations to move, rather than just moving the arm.
- To ensure that the arms are moved rather than moving on their own we start with an addition to the drill. The Respondent touches their pinkie to their body and their index finger to their elbow on the arm touching the Aggressor's weapon arm. That contact MUST never be lost. This forces the Respondent to use body rotation to move their arm rather than an ineffectual arm movement alone.

The Hand Drill Beginning hand position to ensure you use your body to move your arms. Maintain that connect as you move.

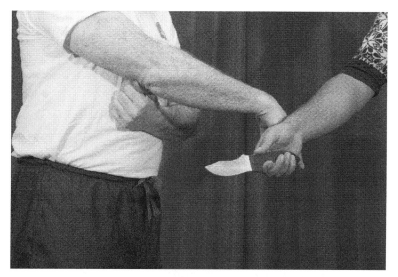

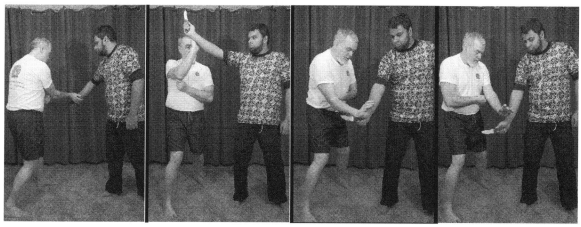

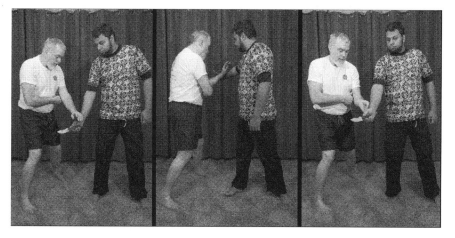

**NOTE THE PRINCIPLES:** The arm on the body ensures that the arms are moved not moving. The other hand sticks and adheres to the weapon arm. BUT ALSO notice the elbow and wrist are now rotating as they move. This rotation is important and it a form of shearing, it can add a great deal of control later.

### Part 2

- Now the Aggressor is not just moving back and forth, but is attempting to cut and stab their partner, while remaining in the restricted movement zone.

- The Respondent keeps their hand or wrist on the weapons hand's wrist and without forcing simply adds to the movement to guide it away from them.

- The Respondent should use hip rotations to move, rather than just moving the arm. You can move your feet too.

- At the start the Respondent should keep that hand connected to the body and their arm, but as they successfully move they can remove it – if they begin to just move their arms without rotation – go back to that connection until they can.

The Respondent's purpose is to use guiding to avoid being cut or stabbed.

The Respondent is NOT trying to push the knife away or stop it, but rather to increase and affect the direction it is already travelling.

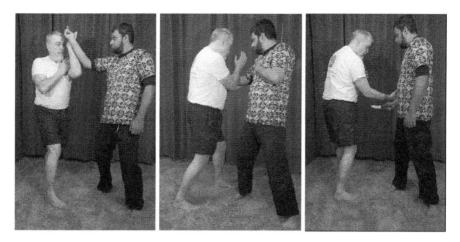

**NOTE THE PRINCIPLES:** We still have the arms are being moved, and we still have sticking and adhering. The elbow and wrist are still rotating. But now we are influencing the movement of the weapon arm – guiding. The purpose of guiding and later leading is so that we can influence the weapon arm to move where we want it without alarming the Aggressor. This is done by not stopping it, which would let them know the strike failed, but to keep it going in a similar direction but not where the Aggressor wanted it to go.

## Part 3

Step Three follows the methodology of Step Two but it adds one factor:

- At some point the movement should **lead** the Aggressor into a small CBI and the Respondent will step in and take control of the weapon arm.

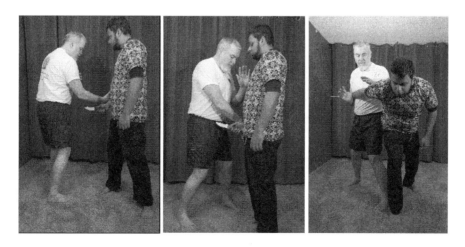

**NOTE THE PRINCIPLES:** All the principles previously mentioned are still being used only now guiding takes a leap. We are not only guiding it where we want it but leading it farther from where it wanted to go and into a "trap" of the CBI. The difference between guiding and leading is subtle. Guiding applies more influence and leading draws the weapon arm off target.

**NOTE:** Okay, this note may just be for Canadians, but I am sure those in other countries with snow or mud will appreciate it as well. **Every Canadian already knows and understands the principles in the Hand Drill.** Every Canadian has pushed a car out of the snow. To push the car out you rock it. You match the roll back and then add pressure to the forward roll and then at some point when it is almost out you drive forward for that last effort. You never try to push forward on the roll back. You do not push with your arms you push with your whole body. When it is time you fully commit. The Hand Drill is based on the very same principles.

In fact, anyone who's ever pushed a child on a swing knows this. Just think about how that is done and ponder.

This drill uses and emphasizes the principle of not alarming your opponent.

# DRILL: Flow Play

Important components:

- Hip Rotation: ALL movement is done using the Hip Rotation.
- The arms and hands DO NOT MOVE they are MOVED by the Hip Rotation.
- Body Avoidance is used from the Tactical Sensitivity Drill.
- Hand Control is used from the Hand Drill.

Begin the Drill:

- Stand close to the partner playing the Aggressor.

For added fun stand with your back to a wall.

- The Aggressor starts slow and builds speed as the Respondent succeeds in clearing the attacks.
- The Aggressor begins to slash and stab at the Respondent.
- The Respondent's goal is to NOT jam, block, or stop the attack, but to guide, redirect, and clear the attack and move their body off the line of force.

Play, increase speed have fun THEN:

- At some point in clearing attack, after attack the Respondent moves in to take control of the weapon arm.
- When done with the Respondent's back against a wall they can still rotate, think sliding along the wall.

Now we are ready for the assaults from really close.

# Assaults From Within One Foot

Assaults from within one foot are small and take little time to deliver; therefore, our response must be equally small and quick.

The Hand Drill will be a vital component of initiating our reactions as we avoid and intercept.

The CBI in its full form disappears and is an exceptionally small and almost blurred reflection of the CBI from large movements.

It is IMPERATIVE that the body movement be a rotation as the hand intercepts the assault, and not merely a movement of the hand.

Once avoided and intercepted, the tactics remain the same depending on if your choice is Distancing Tactics or Closing Tactics.

In the CBI the front hand high and the rear hand is low:

- If the attack is low: rotate and intercept with what will be the rear hand.
- If the attack is high: rotate and intercept with what will be the front hand.

**NOTE:** For these attacks, as it was in the within arm's reach, the Aggressor should attack with the knife coming out of a concealed position.

Now that we are about as close as you can get we will evolve the CBI even smaller to match the shrinking of distance and movement the Aggressor is using – The Evolved CBI:

Avoid and Intercept Attacks from Within One Foot:

**NOTE:** Again, if you work from a right foot forward stance train from a right foot forward stance. Here we are using only a rotation and even from the right stance the rotation is still in the direction described – that will be even more important later.

**TECHNIQUE: Thrusting Stab**

- The Aggressor, from within a foot, thrusts directly at their partner.
- You need to rotate to the right to avoid the blade.
- Because we have learned to move the arm by moving the body we can **begin to intercept the attack with our rear hand AS** we rotate around the thrust leading the weapon arm into the evolved CBI.

In the pictures below a quick rotation engages our hand on the Aggressor's thrust. Because our arms are moved by our body rotation this is one action. If your arms move on their own you must think of trying to coordinate the arms moving with rotating and often end up trying to block the attack. Arms are moved by the rotation = one movement:

**NOTE THE PRINCIPLES:** I didn't wait to the end of these attacks to put this note in because I want you to see the principles NOW and look for them in the rest of the responses. In the second picture above I've shifted as my rotation begins. The shift is into empty space. My right hand has engaged and stuck to the weapon arm. AS I rotate my body my elbow and wrist also rotate shearing and guiding/leading the weapon arm. I am not blocking the attack in anyway, to do so would be to alarm the Aggressor and let him know I am attempting to stop the attack which means he will change. As long as he thinks the attack is working he will continue to stab. When I taught the Knife Defence seminar at the Alberta Peace Officer's 2017 Annual Conference one member couldn't believe that even knowing his partner was going to rotate and guide the weapon arm, even seeing him rotate and no longer be there – HE COULDN'T STOP THE THRUST. Redirecting a committed thrust without prior intent is exceptionally difficult (I'd say impossible but nothing is impossible all the time). Notice the attack is being lead into empty space. This also emphasizes why your partners need to be able to have the intent to stab you as they would in a real-life assault. (As funny as the Jim Carrey skit is, an attack without any intent is "attacking wrong.")

**LOOK FOR THE PRINCIPLES.**

**TECHNIQUE: Back Slash**

- The Aggressor, from within a foot, back slashes at their partner.
- Again, we want to rotate immediately to intercept and cut off the line of force.
- Because we move our arms by moving our body the CBI is already in place as we intercept.

## TECHNIQUE: Over Hand Slash/Stab

- The Aggressor stabs downward at their partner.
- We will rotate to avoid the attack but because this time the attack is higher **our front hand will engage the weapon arm first** to lead it into the evolved CBI AS we rotate.

Our rotation moves our arms immediately engaging our front arm with the weapon arm:

## TECHNIQUE: Uppercut Stab/Slash

- The Aggressor stabs upwards at their partner.
- Once again, we rotate to avoid the attack and this time the line of force is coming in low and from below so **our rear hand engages the weapon arm first** AS we rotate to lead it into the evolved CBI.

Our body rotation immediately engages what will be our rear arm with the weapon arm guiding it as it is lead into the CBI:

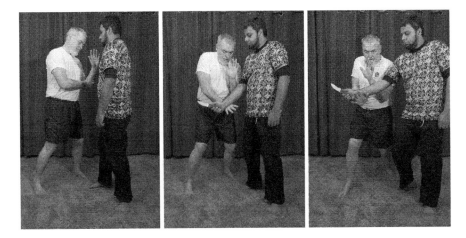

**Distancing Tactics Set**

Once the CBI has been achieved therefore you can proceed to propel the Aggressor away to escape or deploy a weapon.

**Closing Tactics Set:**

You have lead them into the evolved CBI and can now lunge step forward to take control of the weapon arm. From there you can break the arm and/or strike to disable or continue to take them to the ground into a control position.

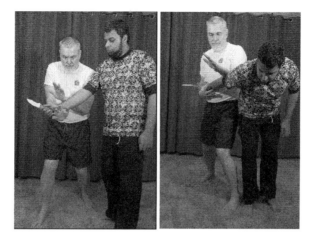

You can also take control using The Clamp:

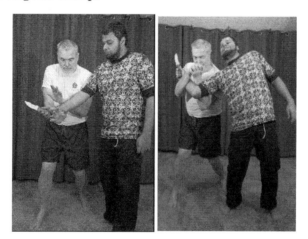

**NOTE:** Within a foot, the "Over Hand Slash/Stab" can take on a deadlier form that often comes from a sheathed knife at their hip, with their hand on the handle appearing to just have their hands on their hips. The knife is drawn up tight along their side to a height just under the chin, and then using the non-weapon hand to back the butt of the handle their stab forward. This could be considered a Thrusting Stab, but the height and manner of deliver makes it more like a low Over Hand Stab. It is vital to rotate off line on this stab, because the braced position of delivery is powerful.

**TECHNIQUE: Front Slash**

- The Aggressor, from within a foot, front slashes at their partner
- Even though the line of force is tight we are going to rotate to the inside using the front hand to intercept and guide the weapon arm into the evolved CBI. Note how the front hand slides down the weapon arm to below the elbow to not only guide but prevent the arm from folding to slash you.

- An option is always to pass the front slash by and move in to catch the returning back slash – SEE Clear the Attack in the next section.

**Distancing Tactics Set**

From the CBI position, you can propel the Aggressor away to escape or deploy a weapon.

**Closing Tactics Set:**

From the Evolved CBI position, you can lunge step to take control of the weapon arm or use the Clamp to lock on and either strike (knees if locked on with the clamp) to disable or take them to the ground into a control position.  The picture below shows the alternative action using the Clamp

**NOTE THE PRINCIPLES:** By now the principles should leap out at you. The Principle of "Control the Distance" is in our tactics. If we want to escape or deploy a weapon we need to have distance between us and the Aggressor so our tactic is to propel away. If we have to disable or are required to control the Aggressor we have to use our closing tactics to get close enough to accomplish it. We move us rather than the Aggressor and we move into empty space because we can do that regardless of how big and strong the Aggressor might be; therefore, size and strength are immaterial to accomplish getting to the strategic position we want. In both propel and take control of the weapon arm we are going to shear into empty space. We will move with our centre to either launch the Aggressor or walk right through empty space taking the weapon arm we have Bone Slaved to us, thus destroying the Aggressor's structure and balance. All the time we will use rotation to add power. When needing to break the weapon arm or take the Aggressor to the ground we are going to sink our mass onto the weapon arm taking advantage of gravity and leverage. If we are using closing tactics we will stick and adhere and do our best to guide and lead the Aggressor into the positions we want without alarming them and allowing them to act before it is too late. You will have seen all of these principles used and if you missed any just look back for them. I know it seems like a lot of stuff going on but it is all done through very simple movements.

**NOTE:** The key to a response equal to the task of dealing with a close quarters attack such as these is engaging the weapon arm immediatelay by touching with the correct hand of the CBI as you rotate. Once you touch simply think of putting your hands together and almost always the CBI is in place.

**Teaching Note:** Before you go on repeat the Left hand Right hand Drill.

## THE GREAT THING

It was said earlier but it is worth repeating. The great thing is that by now you can see that while being outside the weapon arm is preferable, being inside works just fine, too. If you move and end up on the inside of the weapon arm simply take the next steps for being inside. It may not have been the optimum move but you have workable options. So, no matter which way you go (inside weapon arm or outside the weapon arm), the options to survive are there. Never let where you end up, inside or outside, cause you to hesitate or slow down the next step.

# Clear the Attack

Clear the attack will occur for one of four reasons:

1. You intercept the attack, but need to turn them so you do not turn your back to another party.
2. You intercept the attack, but you don't get enough of the CBI done or you feel you will not gain control of the weapon arm so you must clear and regroup
3. You intercept the attack, but feel the Aggressor pulling their weapon arm back and free, preventing you from taking control.
4. You have no opportunity to intercept and must clear the incoming attack away from injuring you.

Reasons 1, 2 and 3 can more precisely be labelled "The Bailout Clears," as you attempted the CBI but it didn't take, or you need to change where the Aggressor will be directed towards and you need to bailout.

Reason 4 more is a tactical intentional action, because no action is abandoned the move is a deliberate clear.

**NOTE:** When clearing the attack, you continue to use the principle of "Move You Not Them" because it will add to the effectiveness of the clear and often results in moving them.

**Control Point:** We will continue to use the Control Point used after implementing the CBI (the back of the weapon arm elbow). It will be our primary control point.

The back of the elbow is chosen in these two circumstances because it allows us to elongate the arm, giving us a longer lever which makes moving the arm across easier. It also prevents the attacker from bending at the elbow and escaping control, which could happen if a control point below the elbow on the forearm were to be chosen.

The redirection of the weapon arm can also employ a specific principle to avoid strength on strength battles or the "knocking" aside and away of the weapon arm. Controlling the weapon arm is also important to this system. We will again use the principle of Shearing to help guide, but a less intrusive form of it.

> **Survival Note:** It is vital that you do not "just" clear the attack and then do nothing. You just continue with the clearing motion to either propel them away or close to finish. Always think of clearing as moving them into the CBI just as in the Hand Drill.

## Clearing the Attack for Reasons 1 and 2 of "The Bailout Clears"

It doesn't matter whether this is for a large attack movement or small attack movement because it happens when step two isn't going to happen and you have to bail.

### TECHNIQUE: Thrusting Stab

The Aggressor thrusts directly at their partner who has intercepted.

The Respondent either has decided they do not want to be facing the direction they rotated or the CBI is not properly in place and they must clear the attack.

The clear is the same for both reasons.

### CLEAR THE WEAPON ARM

The weapon is coming straight in at your body.

You need to get off the line of force and guide it along the same path but extending it farther than the Aggressor wanted to compromise their structure.

This will be described separately, but everything happens at the same time. You will:

- Keeping the rear arm of the CBI down to prevent them from turning the thrust into a back slash, use the upper arm of the CBI to apply guiding pressure on the top of their elbow.
- Rotate to your left (reversing the direction) hooking the control point elbow with your front hand to sweep them downward (or upward if high) and across your body to change sides.
- Control Lunge Step into the arm and body if required to propel them away or to move in to take control of the weapon arm.

CBI on outside of the weapon arm, sweep it down and across to switch to inside:

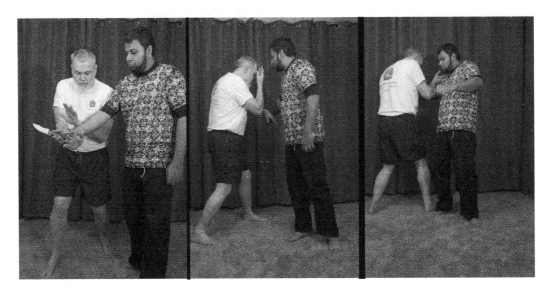

**NOTE THE PRINCIPLES:** You can see that once again the arms are moved they do not move on their own. This is vital is avoiding a knife. If your body and arm movement are not one and the same you will be clearing the knife with your arm AND THEN thinking maybe getting your body out of the way is a smart thing and try to do it as a separate motion. Sweeping the weapon arm across and moving your body off the line is all one motion. It is not two things done at the same time. IT IS ONE THING, if your arms are moved by your body rotation.

**LOOK for this principle and how it is used in the next clearing of the weapon arm.**

**TECHNIQUE: Back Slash**

The Respondent has intercepted the Back Slash and either wants to change the direction they are facing or the CBI is not properly placed so they must clear the attack.

**CLEAR THE WEAPON ARM**

The knife is coming across your body therefore you have to guide and clear it on a similar path.

Obviously, you won't allow it on the path it wants (to gut you).

This will be described separately, but everything happens at the same time. You will:

- Over hook the control point above and THIS TIME in front of the elbow with the front hand of the CBI.
- Hip Rotation turning 180 degrees to your left.
- Hollow the body back and away, just as in the Tactical Sensitivity Drill (as close to this as possible if wearing a vest).

- Use the rear arm of the CBI help deflect the weapon arm lower to miss your body.
- Control Lunge Step into the arm and body if required to propel them away or to move in to take control of the weapon arm.

CBI on outside of the weapon arm, sweep it down and across to switch to inside:

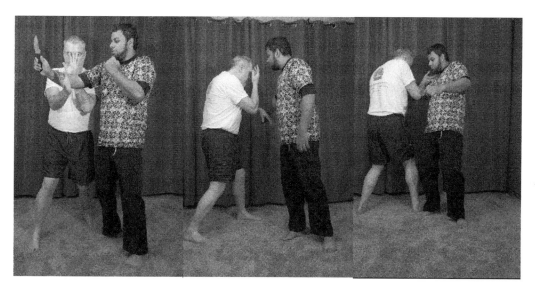

**NOTE THE PRINCIPLES:** One of the important things when clearing is not to clear and do nothing. One way to accomplish this is to guide and lead the weapon arm into the CBI. Look for how the movement and placement of the arms fall right into the CBI.

### TECHNIQUE: Over Hand Slash/Stab

The Over Hand attack has been intercepted but needs to be cleared to change direction or correct a poor CBI.

### CLEAR THE WEAPON ARM

The knife is coming down into your body, therefore, you must guide and clear it on a similar path.

This will be described separately, but everything happens at the same time. You will:

- Over hook the control point above and THIS TIME in front of the elbow with the front hand of the CBI.
- Hip Rotation turning 180 degrees to your left.
- Hollow the body back and away, just as in the Tactical Sensitivity Drill (as close to this as possible if wearing a vest).

- Use the rear arm of the CBI help deflect the weapon arm lower to miss your body.
- As the arm is driven downward it will keep going with your guidance down and on to the rear of the Aggressor.
- Stay connected to the weapon arm and keep it going behind the Aggressor.
- Control Lunge Step into the arm and body if required to propel them away or to move in to take control of the weapon arm.

CBI on outside of the weapon arm, sweep it down and across to switch to inside:

### TECHNIQUE: Uppercut Stab/Slash

The Uppercut Stab has been intercepted but we need to clear to change directions or fix a poor CBI.

### CLEAR THE WEAPON ARM

The weapon is coming up into your body.

You need to get off the line of force and guide it along the same path but extending it farther than the Aggressor wanted to compromise their structure.

This will be described separately, but everything happens at the same time. You will:

- Keep the rear arm of the CBI attached to the weapon arm to help deal with any possible change in direction and to begin to guide the weapon arm higher.

- Use the upper arm of the CBI to apply guiding pressure on the back of their elbow to direct them higher than they wanted to go.
- Rotate left and sweep the weapon arm up and over to be on the inside.
- Control Lunge Step into the arm and body if required to propel them away or to move in to take control of the weapon arm.

CBI on outside of the weapon arm, sweep it up and across to switch to inside:

## TECHNIQUE: Front Slash

You have intercepted the Front Slash but need to clear the weapon arm to change directions or correct for a poor CBI.

## CLEAR THE WEAPON ARM

The knife is coming across your body therefore you have to guide and clear it on a similar path.

Obviously, you won't allow it on the path it wants (to gut you).

This will be described separately, but everything happens at the same time. You will:

- Over hook the control point above and behind the elbow with the front hand of the CBI.
- Hip Rotation turning 180 degrees to your right.
- Hollow the body back and away, just as in the Tactical Sensitivity drill (as close to this as possible if wearing a vest).
- Use the front arm of the CBI help deflect the weapon arm lower to miss your body.

- Control Lunge Step into the arm and body if required to propel them away or to move in to take control of the weapon arm.

CBI on inside of the weapon arm, sweep it down and across to switch to outside.

**NOTE THE PRINCIPLES:** In all the above clears you will have seen the principles of empty space, the arms are moved not moving, sticking, adhering, shearing, rotating, leading and moving with our centre. If you didn't look back over them again.

# Clearing the Attack for Reason 3 of "The Bailout Clears"

It doesn't matter whether this is for a large attack movement or small attack movement because it happens when step two isn't going to happen and they are pulling the knife away and you have to bail.

**TECHNIQUE: Thrusting Stab**

The weapon is coming straight in at your body.

You've gotten off the line of force with hands in the CBI, but the Aggressor has reacted before you could take control of the weapon arm and is retracting the Weapon arm.

This will be described separately, but everything happens at the same time. You will:

- Keeping the rear arm of the CBI down to prevent any them from turning the thrust into a back slash, use the upper arm of the CBI to apply guiding pressure on the back of their elbow.
- As the Aggressor draws the weapon arm back, stick with the front hand of the CBI to the arm above the elbow (C-Clamp position with thumb and index finger) and drive it back taking advantage of their momentum to drive the arm farther back than they wanted.
- Drive into them with a Controlled Lunge Step using your rear hand against their body to propel away from you.

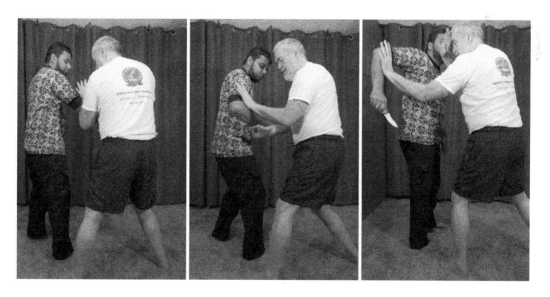

**NOTE THE PRINCIPLES:** All the principles previously mentioned are here but I want to highlight sticking and adhering to that weapon arm. Adhering can also be called following and here when the weapon arm is drawn back you can see we stick and then follow. Adhere is used because we stay attached (stuck) to the weapon arm. At this point we adhere and stick to take it back farther than the Aggressor wants to as we strike to their head. We are not in control of the weapon arm but we are interfering. It is not a great place to try and go for control. It may be after we strike to disable but at the moment caught in the picture above disable is the safest path.

**TECHNIQUE: Back Slash**

They are retracting the strike

At the same time you will:

- Keeping the rear arm of the CBI down to prevent any them from coming back again with a second back slash, use the upper arm of the CBI to apply guiding pressure on the back of their elbow.
- As the Aggressor draws the weapon arm back, stick with the front hand of the CBI to the arm above the elbow taking advantage of their momentum to and drive it back into their body to pin it against them.
- Drive into them with a Controlled Lunge Step using your front hand against their elbow to propel away from you.

**NOTE THE PRINCIPLES:** I am sure you can all see the sticking and adhering now, but do you see the use of empty space? Look at the change in position of the Aggressor's shoulder from the second picture above to the third. The shear as we moved in (with our centre) is not into the Aggressor's structure instead it is angle up into the empty space behind the Aggressor's head.

**TECHNIQUE: Over Hand Slash/Stab**

As they retract the strike you will:

- Keeping the rear arm of the CBI down to prevent any them from stabbing downward again and hooking into your body, use the front arm of the CBI to follow the Aggressor's weapon arm back up moving your hand under and on the back of their elbow.
- As the Aggressor draws the weapon arm back up for another stab, stick with the front hand of the CBI to the arm above the elbow and drive it back and upwards taking advantage of their momentum to drive the arm higher and farther back than they wanted.
- Drive into them with a Controlled Lunge Step using your front hand against their elbow to propel away from you.
- The rear hand can assist in pushing on the elbow or deliver elbow strikes.

**NOTE THE PRINCIPLES:** Note how as I adhere (follow) the attack back I drive the elbow up into empty space.

## TECHNIQUE: Uppercut Stab/Slash

As they retract the strike you will:

- Keeping the rear arm of the CBI down to prevent them from turning the thrust into a back slash, use the front arm of the CBI to apply guiding pressure on the back of their elbow.
- As the Aggressor draws the weapon arm back up for another stab, stick with the rear hand of the CBI to the arm above the elbow (C-Clamp position with thumb and index finger) and drive it back and upwards taking advantage of their momentum to drive the arm higher and farther back than they wanted.
- Drive into them with a Controlled Lunge Step using your rear hand against their body to propel away from you.

**NOTE THE PRINCIPLES:** Can you see how empty space is used to drive the arm back?

## TECHNIQUE: Front Slash

As they retract the strike:

- Keeping the rear arm of the CBI down to prevent them from shifting to a lower slash.
- As the Aggressor draws the weapon arm back, stick with the rear hand of the CBI to the arm THIS TIME below the elbow (C-Clamp position with thumb and index finger) and drive it back taking advantage of their momentum to drive the arm farther back than they wanted.
- Drive into them with a Controlled Lunge Step using your rear hand against their body to propel away from you.

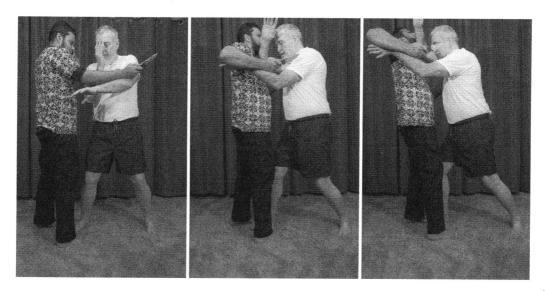

**NOTE THE PRINCIPLES:** Can you see how empty space is used to drive the elbow back as I step in moving my centre? I am not moving the arm into the Aggressor's structure or strength.

In the next two operant conditioning drills the Aggressor as much as possible wants to retract out of the CBI and the Respondent must compensate. In addition, the Respondent can decide to switch side by clearing simply to practice.

# DRILL: Operant Conditioning #5

- The partners stand within arm's reach.
- The Aggressor will have a knife hidden from view and then **IN SLOW MOTION** pull it and attack with any of the main attacks: Thrusting Stab, Front slash, Back Slash, Over Hand Slash/Stab or Uppercut Stab/Slash.
- Do at least one of every FIVE attacks with the knife in the left hand.
- The Aggressor may try to retract the knife after they attack.
- The Respondent can choose to switch position after the CBI.
- If the Respondent doesn't get a good CBI they should clear and finish.
- Trade roles.

# DRILL: Operant Conditioning #6

- The partners stand within arm's reach.
- The Respondent closes their eyes.
- The Aggressor will have a knife hidden from view and then **IN SLOW MOTION** pull it and attack with any of the main attacks: Thrusting Stab, Front slash, Back Slash, Over Hand Slash/Stab, or Uppercut Stab/Slash)

JUST BEFORE THEY MOVE, THE AGGRESSOR WILL SAY BEGIN.

- **WHEN THE AGGRESSOR SAYS BEGIN THE RESPONDENT MAY OPEN THEIR EYES AND ACT.**
- Do at least one of every FIVE attacks with the knife in the left hand.
- The Aggressor may try to retract the knife after they attack.
- The Respondent can choose to switch position after the CBI.
- If the Respondent doesn't get a good CBI they should clear and finish.
- Trade roles.

# Steps for Reason 4

There is no achieving the CBI in reason 4, because the attack is too sudden or fast to intercept, or you have chosen to let it go by and therefore we need to pass it by in hopes to be able to disrupt the Aggressor's balance or get a second chance to intercept.

In this we want to think back to the Tactical Sensitivity Drill and the Hand Drill as to how we guided or lead the attack by. Only now, do it against large movement attacks and then small movement attacks rather than the blade on the body as it was done in the Tactical Sensitivity Drill.

### Clear the Weapon Arm Reason #4

It is far less likely in large attacks you will be clearing the attack, because you could not intercept. As previously described, it is more likely the intercept didn't get transitioned to control or projection.

There is the chance that you have been distracted and only pick up the large attack at the last moment, but it is more likely the attack is fast and from in very close (minimum an arm's reach and more likely closer).

The ambush surprise has meant the best you can do is clear the weapon without injury, allowing you to close for control.

You can also use this clear to choose which direction you rotate. There may be another party you do not want to turn your back on.

IMPORTANT POINT:

Whenever possible do not "just clear."

- Clear and do something.
- Clear and propel to get distance.
- Clear and stick to move in for control.
- Lead them into the CBI.

Never just clear unless there is no option or you are going to have to immediately defend again from the next attack.

You will find that the Hand Drill is vital for clearing sudden assaults and dealing with assaults closer than an arm's reach, within one foot.

The pictures below illustrate the tactical clear of a front slash sweeping it across to take the CBI position on the outside of the weapon arm:

The pictures below illustrate the tactical clear of a back slash sweeping it across to take the CBI position on the inside of the weapon arm:

While not "always" once you pass a slash by the next logical attack is for the Aggressor to slash back in the opposite direction; therefore, your logical next move is to preapre to meet this reversal with the CBI. This logic helps with an Aggressor who closes in with quick back and forth slashes.

**Teaching Note:** Watch for this interesting oddity: when the slash is coming at a person's midsection they easily grasp sweeping the attack by and pulling their belly back out of the way but when the attack is high, suddenly, they want to block with a clash before clearing. The principles in a clear are to not clash but sweep and encourage the attack to go by AS you pull your body out of the way. Nothing changes in a high clear. Sweep the attack by and pull your head back out of the way.

**DRILL:** Return the previous Play Flow Drill against the wall and apply what you have learned about clear to avoidance and taking control.

**This drill is all about giving you time to play and find a real enjoyment in using the principles to manipulate the Aggressor. A fantastic learning tool but remember it is a micro moment skill set drill and do not do it so much you start playing around when you up the intensity of the assaults in Practice.**

# How to Cut The Time between Intercepting the Weapon Arm and Either Propel or Controlling the Weapon Arm – The Principle of Tendon Power

One principle only mentioned once so far is Tendon Power. The human body is a big ball of elastics and one way to tap into it quickly is to think of having springs on the bottom of your feet. (If you google Spring Shoes you can get images of one's people created). When we rotate (i.e. To the right) we are driving our mass to the right and it will be absorbed onto our right foot. If we visualize our right foot having a spring under it we can absorb into it and bounce off that spring immediately into the next tactic – propel the Aggressor or right through the weapon arm. It is a powerful quick action adding that natural spring. It cuts the time between avoid and intercept and the next tactic eliminating any delay. This is important and an absolute necessity when dealing with the repetitive stabs of the assassinations.

## Assassinations – Sewing Machine Stabs

**Survival Note:** ALWAYS remember one response to the sudden assassination attempt after avoiding while intercepting is to PROPEL the Aggressor away from you. That option will not be shown below, but propel can be your planned tactic, or if you avoided with the intention of getting control of an arm but can't you can ALWAYS step in a propel them away. Keep that in mind.

Now we deal with the major league 90 mph fast ball and everything you learned is going to be needed. You will find the rotation that has been emphasized is your survival key and without it you will die in training and in the street.

As before your stance left or right is immaterial, it is the direction of the rotation that is important (Left handed assaults always reverse the rotation direction.)

Assassination attacks are shocking and quick.

There is a mental process needed to add reaction speed to your response to these sudden violent responses.

## The OCR "Oh crap I don't want to be stabbed."

The OCR is a natural reaction to an attempted stabbing and we are going to tap into this response.

As odd as this may sound, your mind is your most powerful weapon. For the assassinations, I want you to think of that withdrawing of the body from the line of force and placing your arms to protect. I want a retreat step with a rotation. As you move, take that step of thinking "Oh no I don't want to be stabbed." (Thinking OH CRAP – MOVE might be enough...) You will be surprised at what this focused intent will add to your movement.

In most cases, the Aggressor's non-weapon arm becomes involved to grab and control the Respondent. They could be grabbing clothing or hooking behind the head to pull into the knife or across in front of the body to hold the Respondent off and prevent them from getting to the weapon arm.

The other change that most often accompanies an assassination is the use of the knife: cutting disappears, as do committed thrusts. Stabs inflict life threatening wounds and committed thrusts allow more options for gaining control of the weapon arm. The attacks become quick short thrusts driving in and out like the actions of a sewing machine.

**IMPORTANT:** When the Aggressor is in front of you, you must rotate so you are on the outside of the weapon arm on sewing machine stabs, because if they succeed in retracting the stab and you are on the inside (and remain there) you will lose any chance of maintaining contact and control and they can alter where they stab making it almost impossible to stop. IF you do rotate to the inside you will have to work at timing another thrust to rotate and switch to the outside as you intercept but keep your arms in place because the next thrust in a sewing machine stab comes quickly.

**Teaching Note:** After working each assassination type right handed – switch and work against a left-hand attack.

## Non-weapon Arm Grabbing the Respondent's Clothes

- The Aggressor has the knife in the saber grip and reaches up to grab the Respondent by the clothes with the non-weapon arm. They begin to use a sewing machine motion to rapidly and repeatedly stab at the Respondent's lower abdomen as they pull them in with the non-weapon arm's grip on the clothes.
- The Respondent must ignore the grab, because that form of grab cannot prevent you from dropping back with your right foot and performing a quick Hip and Foot Rotation to the right
- You **MUST** rotate so that you are fully facing right to survive. Half measures will get you killed.

**As you are doing the hip rotation** with your left arm high and right arm low, perform a very small CBI. You must do this with your hip rotation. Just as with the attacks from within one foot you will **begin the intercept with the rear (low) hand of the CBI.**

Think: "Oh no I don't want to be stabbed" and watch yourself get out of the way of this dangerous attack.

- You must be perpendicular to the weapon arm and need to **Take Control of the Weapon Arm.**
- Let the front hand or forearm hook behind the Elbow Control Point of the weapon arm.
- Continue to rotate and guide them past you so you can then proceed with the normal take control of the weapon arm.
- They will attempt to pull the weapon arm back to continue the sewing machine stabs. You can prevent their retraction with that hook behind the control point. An interesting mechanical note is the fact they are drawing back and driving forward and this compresses the tendons on the draw back and as they

thrust forward it releases and propels them farther than they intended. Because their intent is to draw and stab again it is difficult for them to change this intent quickly enough to stop because you've got their control point.

HOWEVER, sometimes the retraction is so strong you cannot stop them. In that case, simply go with it, maintaining contact which will result in one of three ends:

1. They do not pull back far enough to break free of your hook and their own action helps to propel them forward. You will rotate again adding to the propel guiding them past you and farther which will allow you to get control of the weapon arm.

2. They pull so far back you cannot maintain the hook behind the weapon arm. In this case continue to adhere and follow the weapon arm being drawn back but let your hand slide to the front of the weapon arm taking a C- clamp position (web area between your index and thumb forming the "C") in the crux of their elbow. This will block a forward thrust and allow you drive into them and to IF they try to escape this block by retracting back even farther, follow and control and strike but if they pull back so far you lose contact on the control point then allow you hand to slide down in the C-Clamp position to control the wrist. And strike repeatedly to their head with elbows until the threat has stopped.

The grab, even done with force pulling you, cannot prevent you from rotating.

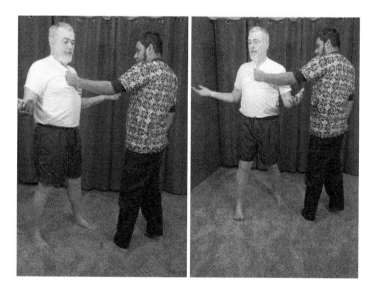

**NOTE THE PRINCIPLE:** We are simply rotating and using empty space. The Aggressor's grip leaves all kinds of empty space that we can rotate to and never encounter their structure or an obstacle.

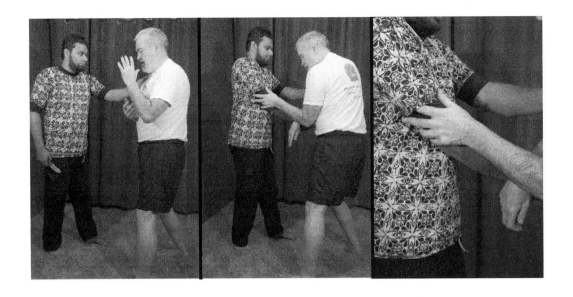

STICK and do the same rotation as always:

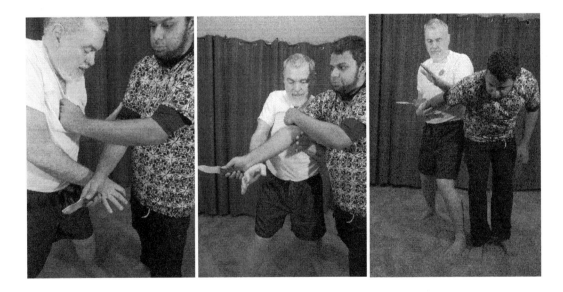

If they do succeed in retracting the strike, then follow and get to the C Clamp position:

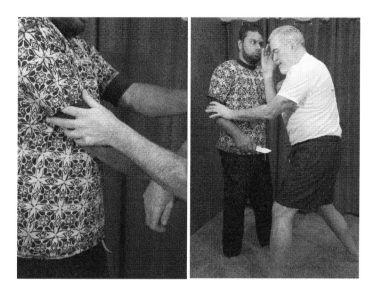

**NOTE THE PRINCIPLES:** On assassination sewing machine stabs the principles of stick and adhere are vital. We need to attach to that weapon arm and if we cannot guide / lead it right away because of the stabbing actions we need to follow and take the elbow into empty space farther back that they intended which weakens their structure and we can drive forward – I highly recommend striking them repeatedly in the head as you do so with your right hand or better, elbow.

**Stop the threat**

This depends where they end up.

If you succeed in turning them you will be in the CBI position and can lunge step forward to take control of the weapon arm or use the Clamp, either will place you in position to disable with strikes or take them to the ground into a control position.

If you have failed to turn them, strike repeatedly until the threat is stopped or continue to follow the retracting weapon arm stepping into it pressing it back even further and allow your front hand to slip down to the wrist, and with the left hand C-Clamped on the elbow wrist place your right rear hand on the elbow control point (front of elbow) drop pulling it (and them) to the ground.

The Aggressor is retracting the strike. You rotate back sticking and adhering to the weapon arm, allowing your front hand to rotate to the front of the weapon arm's elbow:

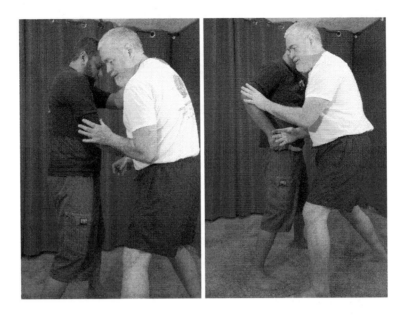

You continue to move forward and press on the weapon arm causing the Aggressor to pull it back farther and as he does you follow the motion slipping your front hand down to the wrist:

You have moved the weapon arm back off the Aggressor's base and over empty space. Gripping the weapon arm, you drop your centre, dropping your mass on the arm driving the Aggressor into the ground:

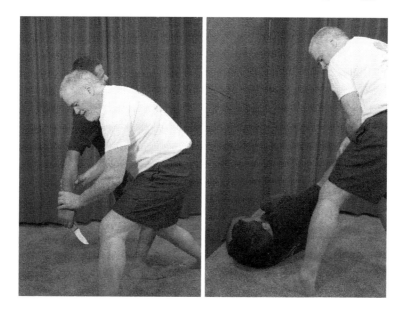

**NOTE THE PRINCIPLES**: We use sticking and adhering to stay with the weapon arm. We move with our centre so driving the weapon arm back farther than the Aggressor wants to go is a powerful movement and you will note the arm is pressed back into empty space. We then have the weapon arm off the Aggressor's base over empty space and we use gravity sinking our centre to drop him to the ground.

# DRILL: Operant Conditioning #7

**Note:** This begins as soft adrenaline training beginning with the attacks being done slowly BUT as the Respondent succeeds you repeat the attack at ever increasing speed until it is a full out attack = Hard Adrenaline Training.

**Part 1** Not Completely Operant Conditioning (See Survival Note)

- The Aggressor gets into the assault position with their non-weapon hand grabs the Respondent's clothes and begins the sewing machine assault.
- The Respondent defends.

**Survival Note:** Starting by allowing them to grab you is not a thing to ingrain; it is bad for survival. Why start in that position? Because the assassination is a surprise the grab is often your first cue to move. So we train it here BUT, be consciously uncomfortable allowing them into the position to practice (As my friend Rick Bottomley would say.) Make grabbing you as artificial as possible.

**Part 2**

Now we begin close with the Aggressor going for the grab and stab and the Respondent gets to move the moment the Aggressor starts to go for the grab – THEY DO NOT HAVE TO WAIT UNTIL GRABBED.

- The Aggressor grabs and stabs.
- The Respondent initiates the defence the MOMENT the grab is initiated NOT after they are grabbed.

# Non-Weapon Arm Grabbing Behind the Respondent's Head

- The Aggressor has the knife in the saber grip and reaches up to grab the Respondent around the back of the head with the non-weapon arm. They begin to use a sewing machine motion to rapidly and repeatedly stab at the Respondent's lower abdomen as they pull them in with the non-weapon arm's grip behind the head.
- The Respondent must ignore the neck grab. Allow yourself to drop back with your right foot and performs a Hip Rotation to the right ending with you perpendicular to the weapon arm.

**IMPORTANT:** It is vital that when you rotate you LOOK UP to prevent being pulled forward which will impede the rotation.

**As you are doing the hip rotation** with your left arm high and right arm low perform a very small CBI **beginning the intercept with the rear (low) hand of the CBI.**

Again, use your mind and the thought process: "Oh no I don't want to be stabbed."

Ending the threat will be accomplished just as in the previous assassination variation depending on where the Aggressor ends up.

Note that when grabbed behind the head if we simply rotate and look up as we do they cannot pull us over.

**NOTE THE PRINCIPLES:** This is an interesting use of empty space. As we rotate we look up – to empty space. Because the head rotation is into empty space it succeeds and makes it exceptionally difficult for the Aggressor to pull our head down like they want to. The reasons for this are three-fold. First just as we press down on the head when pinning on the ground pulling down on our head disconnects us from using our strong back muscles, by looking up we continue to access them. Second with our head up the rotation moves us away from their strength line. Third, our rotation with our head up draws the Aggressor out and raises their shoulder weakening their structure.

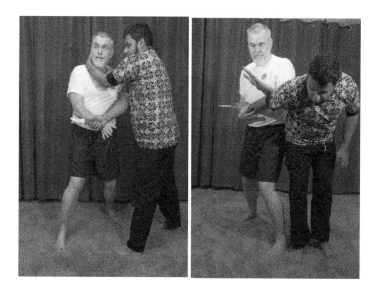

# DRILL: Operant Conditioning #8

**Note:** This begins as soft adrenaline training, with the attacks being done slowly. BUT as the Respondent Partner succeeds, you repeat the attack at ever increasing speed until it is a full out attack (Hard Adrenaline Training).

**Part 1**

- The Aggressor gets into the assault position with their non-weapon hand behind the head of the Respondent and begins the sewing machine assault.
- The Respondent defends.

**Part 2**

Now we begin close with the Aggressor going for the grab and stab and the Respondent gets to move the moment the Aggressor starts to go for the grab – THEY DO NOT HAVE TO WAIT UNTIL GRABBED.

- The Aggressor grabs and stabs.
- The Respondent initiates the defence the MOMENT the grab is initiated NOT after they are grabbed.

# Non-Weapon Arm to Brace Across the Respondent's Chest to Hold Them Away From the Weapon (They Could Also Grab Your Clothing)

In all other cases, we have addressed intercepting or clearing the weapon arm; however, in this case that is exceptionally difficult, because the bracing arm prevents both interception, passing of the weapon arm and getting deep enough to get to the control point without taking damage – THAT is why they do it.

In this case, you must treat the bracing arm as the hindrance to your survival and you are going to control and use it in the same manner you would clear the weapon arm.

- The Aggressor has the knife in the saber grip and reaches up across the chest of the Respondent with the non-weapon arm bracing them away from the weapon arm (Often clothing is grabbed for more control). They begin to use a sewing machine motion to rapidly and repeatedly stab at the Respondent's lower abdomen.
- The Respondent must ignore the weapon arm and focus on the non-weapon bracing arm.

**As you are doing the hip rotation** to your left with your right arm high and left arm low perform the CBI bracing your front outside forearm on the NON-weapon arm's control point.

- Rear hand immediately under hooks the non-weapon arm for more control and potential arm break.
- **Continue to rotate until you are at 180 degrees from the weapon arm. If you do not continue to rotate until you reach 180 degrees they can still reach and stab you. This is vital.**
- You are now perpendicular (at 90 degrees) to the NON-weapon arm simply step straight forward into the empty space and **Take Control of the NON-Weapon Arm.**
- Your left (front) forearm is above their elbow. Step through their arm shearing forward with the outside edge of your forearm. This movement drives them forward and down disconnecting the shoulder with the back. (Down for control as opposed to up to propel.)
- As they are moved, continue to shear your forearm over and move you to the non-weapon arm.
- Allow the step to move you to the arm not on the control point (rear right arm). As you step bend the elbow bringing the arm up thumb to chest hand perpendicular to the chest. Your wrist bone will come to contact with the non-weapon arm. Thinking of squeezing bone to bone squeeze all the air and space out from between your wrist and the weapon arm (wring out the towel).
- With the Controlled Lunge Step, you will be dropping your centre slightly sink onto the non-weapon arm and end the control lunge step with a rotation.

## Stop the threat

This is a really bad place so there is a reasonable basis for doing damage immediately (as there is in most knife defence situations); therefore, when you rotate out to control the non-weapon arm do it with the intent of not only getting control of the arm but to abruptly continue the two-way action on the elbow to break it.

You can also slam them to the ground so that they are face down and cannot reach you with the weapon arm. Here, depending on the remaining threat, you can strike and/or break the arm to disable, or continue to control them. But remember even though the Aggressor is pinned on the ground, you do not have control of the weapon arm and should be prepared to disengage and escape or disable.

Safety Note: In training take is slow because this move done quickly can break the non-weapon arm. Not a problem in the street but it may limit willing training partners.

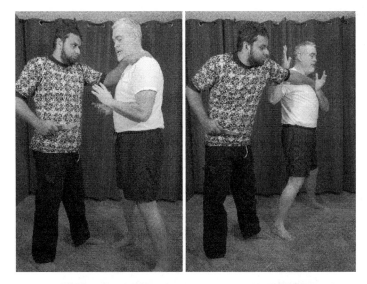

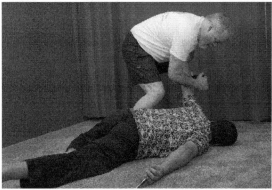

**NOTE THE PRINCIPLES:** The Aggressor's non-weapon arm is braced against us. The purpose is to hold us off so that we cannot reach the knife as they stab us. But behind us is empty space and the brace cannot stop us from rotating back and out. The brace only stops us moving forward.

When rotating out you must rotate far enough to be in-line with the Aggressor or they can still reach you to stab. You can check your position by seeing if you are in a line with the Aggressor (as shown below):

# DRILL: Operant Conditioning #9

**Note:** This begins as soft adrenaline training beginning with the attacks being done slowly, BUT as the Respondent succeeds you repeat the attack at ever increasing speed until it is a full out attack (Hard Adrenaline Training).

**Part 1**

- The Aggressor gets into the assault position with their non-weapon hand across the Respondent's chest bracing them away or grabbing their clothing to brace them away and begins the sewing machine assault.
- The Respondent defends.

**Part 2**

Now we begin close with the Aggressor going for the grab and stab and the Respondent gets to move the moment the Aggressor starts to go for the grab – THEY DO NOT HAVE TO WAIT UNTIL GRABBED.

- The Aggressor grabs and stabs.
- The Respondent initiates the defence the MOMENT the grab is initiated NOT after they are grabbed.

# Hand Shake Assassination

A very deliberate and targeted assassination is the "Handshake Assassination."

- The Aggressor holds the knife in their left hand hidden behind their leg.
- As they shake your hand they pull you in against them stabbing repeatedly to your side and back.

For those who might ask "why would I ever shake the hand of a suspect or person I was questioning?" let me tell you a story.

One night about 2:00 a.m. in the morning, I received a call from the police. One of my teenage children who was struggling at that time was now in their custody, on a street corner in cuffs, and they wanted me to come get my child. In the background, I could hear my child screaming at them that I was a black belt and when I got down here I was going to kick their %^%$ teeth down their throats. Nice.

When I arrived, I found two officers and to say they were slightly pumped on adrenaline would be an understatement. When I approached it was tense. I immediately put out my hand and before he knew it the officer was shaking it.

I could see two things run across his face: "What the.... And, okay, he's alright."

I was thinking, "Damn, I have his weapon hand." Sorry, that's just how my mind works.

The point is, there was no way that officer was expecting a handshake but before he could stop himself he was shaking my hand.

If I had wanted to hurt him the opportunity to try was there. Of course, I was using the hand shake to calm things down and let the officer know there wasn't going to be a problem.

Prior to this, I'd had to deal with many extremely upset people who wanted to verbally rip a strip off of me, and so one of my techniques to engage them and calm them down was to walk up and offer my hand.

When they took it, and they always took it, I gave them a warm handshake. They were always upset at themselves for taking my hand and almost always felt now they had to proceed a little less upset, at least for a while.

What this shows is that we are habituated to shake a hand when it is offered, so much so we do it without thinking.

Habits are powerful and there isn't a gap between cue and response (read "Addendum #1: Operant Conditioning to Habit Response"). How do we handle this if this if an Aggressor wanting to do us harm?

**Change your habit.**

You could stop shaking hands, or change how you do it. Alter your habit.

1.  When you shake hands, start angling yourself slightly off line away from their left hand. (Slightly, enough to be off line but not to be weird.)
2.  Start being very friendly and shake with two hands.

From this position, you have easy control over their right hand and can rotate to your right lifting their right hand out and up taking control of them.

From there, you simply finish with one of the set out options but remember you are already engage and gripping them so Closing Tactics are in order, control or disable are your options.

# DRILL: Operant Conditioning #10

**Note:** This begins as soft adrenaline training beginning with the attacks being done slowly, BUT as the Respondent succeeds you repeat the attack at ever increasing speed until it is a full out attack (Hard Adrenaline Training).

- The Aggressor offers their hand to shake with the weapon in their left hand tucked out of sight behind their left thigh.

- The Respondent shakes hands but in the recommended tactical position.
- The Aggressor attempts to stab them repeated in the side and back while pulling in on the hand.
- The Respondent uses their two hands on the Aggressor's hand to rotate, stretch out and lift the Aggressor's non-weapon hand.
- The Respondent defends.

# ONE LAST ASSASSINATION STYLE

This one comes from the research done by Randy King of KPC Self Defence in Edmonton Alberta. A style of assault becoming common is the overhand stab but the Aggressor keeps their elbow tight to the body as they stab in a short sewing machine manner. The knife is held in the ice pick grip and if they know what they are doing they will "cap it." Cap it simply means to place your thumb on top of the butt of the handle to help prevent sliding down the blade when stabbing. Randy's constant research into common assaults is what make KPC one of the best self defence schools in the world.

## Assassination: Overhand Stab with elbow tight and done in sewing machine like multiple stabs.

The Aggressor will grab you in some manner with the non-weapon hand to control you (see previous assassination styles). They will stab down either into your chest or hooking slightly to your back (if attacking from the side) with quick repetitive stabs while keeping their elbow close to their body.

Rotate to your right to get outside the weapon arm.

It is important to get the front hand of the CBI over the weapon arm and the rear arm under.

Because the elbow is held so tight into the body it may be impossible to get that control point so make sure the front hand of the CBI is across the weapon arm's forearm to interfere with repetitive stabs and immediately lock the Clamp onto their forearm and step driving with your centre (backwards or forwards) to take the arm and elbow away from their body and then DROP onto the arm forcing them to hit the ground.

If you moved to the inside you can still make the same response to control the arm with the clamp; however, it is more dangerous because the Aggressor can rotate their wrist to face the blade towards you. While they can do this when you are on the outside the angle is different and less threatening.

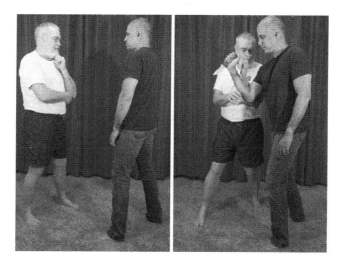

It is vital that you have the front hand of the CBI not only up but allow it to extend over the weapon arm.

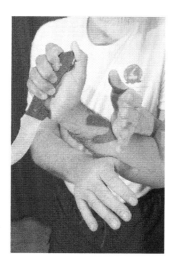

The reason we want to be here is because they will withdraw the blade to strike again (remember they are stabbing in a sewing machine manner) and when they do this will allow us to rotate and follow in and apply the Clamp.

We begin to rotate, slide forward and sink onto the elbow to begin breaking the Aggressor's structure (note in the picture below how it has moved the Aggressor backwards – he was in a left stance and now is bent and in a right stance:

We will then step through for a takedown using the Clamp as our Bone Slaving tool.

**NOTE THE PRINCIPLES:** I am sure you have seen the use of empty space and the bone slaving but the principle to highlight here is elasticity. When we place our front hand over the weapon arm and the Aggressor forcefully pulls it back to stab again we do not resist but use that pull to move into a deep locked Clamp.

# Operant Conditioning Drill #11

Note: Just as in all the assassination drills this begins as soft adrenaline training beginning with the attacks being done slowly, BUT as the Respondent succeeds you repeat the attack at ever increasing speed until it is a full out attack (Hard Adrenaline Training). Use a safe training knife to get very aggressive and real.

**Part 1**
- The Aggressor gets into the assault position with their non-weapon hand grabbing the Respondent begins the over hand sewing machine assault.
- The Respondent defends.

**Part 2**

Now we begin close with the Aggressor going for the grab and begins to over hand stab and the Respondent gets to move the moment the Aggressor starts to go for the grab – THEY DO NOT HAVE TO WAIT UNTIL GRABBED.

- The Aggressor grabs and stabs.
- The Respondent initiates the defence the MOMENT the grab is initiated NOT after they are grabbed.

# NOW FOR THE HARD PART

Up until now we have had the aggressor in front of us. This allows us to learn the skills we need and how to apply the principles that we have learned. But, as I said at the start, attacks often come from the side. We will cover this under "Situations" as well, but what about in an assault?

Oddly, assaults from the side when the non-weapon hand isn't being utilized by the Aggressor seems easier, so it would have been nice if that had been the reality, but unfortunately that isn't reality. Reality is that the Aggressor will use the non-weapon arm to grab and attempt to control you as they sewing machine stab and if the weapon is in the hand towards your back they more commonly will curve the stabs into your back and kidneys.

## Problem:

Picture the Aggressor standing at your left side. Their left (non-weapon) arm has grabbed your left shoulder. Their weapon arm (right) is going to stab repeatedly into your back. Regardless of how they grab you with their left hand it is exceptionally difficult to get to the outside of the weapon arm. The grab prevents you from moving to get deep enough on the outside to get to the control point (elbow). The grab also prevents you from trying to rotate to the inside of the weapon arm.

The questions become which way do we rotate? What do we control?

## Solution:

Fortunately, we have explored an alternative when dealing with the arm braced across our body – rotating to take control of the non-weapon arm. This will also be a technique used here, because there is a commonality in the best option.

The solution is to rotate to the side of the body you feel contact.

You are grabbed (or worse stabbed) on your RIGHT side – you rotate RIGHT regardless of how you are grabbed or which hand the knife is in.

You are grabbed (or worse stabbed) on your LEFT side – you rotate LEFT regardless of how you are grabbed or which hand the knife is in.

YOU MUST ROTATE 180 DEGREES TO FACE THE OPPOSITE DIRECTION FROM WHERE YOU STARTED. This will put you 90 degrees to the arm you want to control.

When you rotate you take control of the arm you contact regardless of whether it is the weapon arm or the non-weapon arm.

Propel the Aggressor away or disable the arm or go for control.

**Left Side Right Handed Aggressor – Rotate to your LEFT**

The moment we feel contact from our left side we rotate to our left engaging the CBI on whichever arm is closest to us:

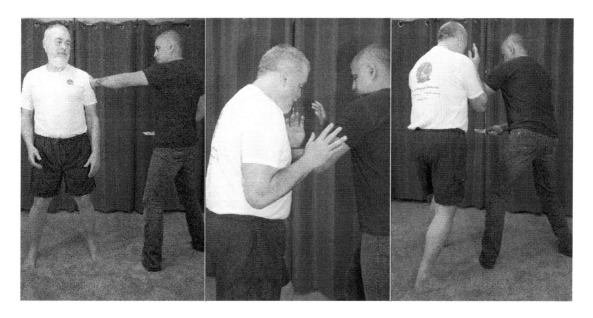

Contact has been made and we immediately take a controlled lunge step forward shearing into the non-weapon arm to off balance the aggressor and drive them to the ground. A common reaction to an impending face plant is for the Aggressor to put their free hand down to prevent it (the weapon arm):

We don't have control of the weapon arm so we immediately stretch the Aggressor out face down and use the non-weapon arm to pin them to the ground. You can even place your knee on top of their elbow for control or a quick arm break:

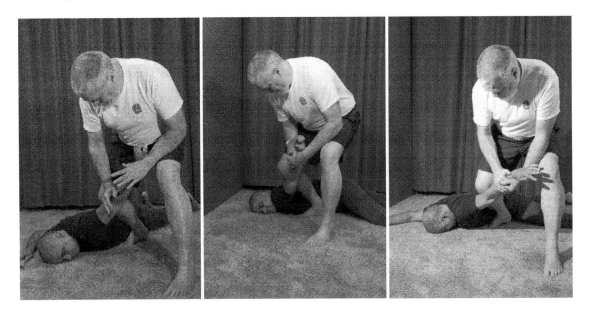

**Using the Clamp and Stepping Back to get control of the Non-weapon arm:**

The moment we feel contact we rotate in the direction of the contact and form the CBI:

We have contact and we want to take control with the clamp, so we rotate back to the right and into the clamp and take a step back with our right leg swinging the clamp under and into our body with a left rotation (you can see how that buckles the aggressor's legs and twists the weapon arm away from us):

Now that we have their balance we use a rear sliding control lunge step rotating back to the right to rip the Aggressor out and off their base to the ground to be placed in control. Knee on the head and their arm in a breakable position:

## Left Side, Left handed Aggressor – Rotate to your LEFT.

Once again, the moment contact is made we rotate to the side of contact and as shown below shear over the weapon arm to take control and finish:

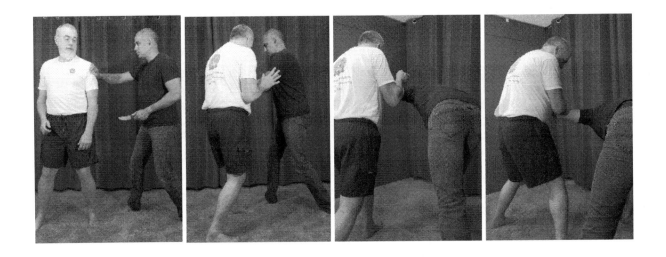

**Alternative response using The Clamp:** The moment the Aggressor contact we rotate to the side of contact then rotate back to the right to lock on the Clamp and break their structure and take their balance:

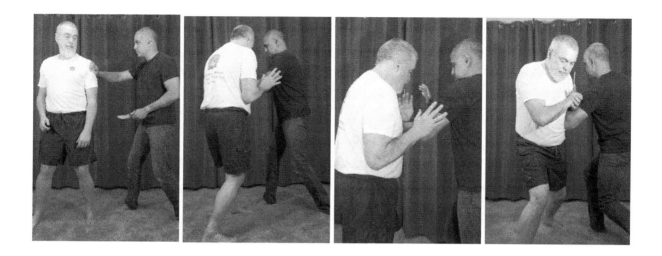

We take a sliding lunge step backwards dragging the Aggressor with us off their base and then sink on their elbow to drop them to the ground:

**Right Side, Right Handed Aggressor**: At the moment of contact rotate to the side of contact and take control of the arm closest to you and finish as described previously in assassinations from the other side - Rotate to your RIGHT:

**Right Side, Left Handed Aggressor**: Again, at the moment of contact rotate to the side of contact and take control of the arm closest to you and finish as described previously in assassinations from the other side - Rotate to your RIGHT:

By simply rotating to the side you are grabbed makes operantly conditioning this response a simpler process.

**NOTE THE PRINCIPLES:** As always, we need to not just think of these movements as techniques to memorize but actions implementing principles. We rotate to the side of contact – why? We do so because no matter how they grab us with the non-weapon arm rotating to the side of contact is possible because we rotate through empty space. They can use their non-weapon arm to interfere and block our rotation in the other direction. Once we have rotated we are in our balanced flexible structure. We again look for empty space to move into either shearing forward through the arm we are controlling or bone slaving the arm to us and using gravity to drop back. Both actions move through empty space and use gravity to add mass and break the balance and structure of the Aggressor. All the principles we have learned and applied are used here against these deadly assaults.

## Assassinations From Behind

Sorry I don't have any Ninja secrets or Spider Sense to give you here. If you are caught unaware from behind the first indication you have you are being attacked will be contact either from the non-weapon arm or you are stabbed. The question is what to do then.

As you will see in the situation when there is a knife to your back the recommendation is to rotate to your right. Most people are right handed so most of the time you will contact the weapon arm. If it is a left handed attack you will contact the non-weapon arm and, as always either propel away, disable the arm and the Aggressor or go for control.

From Behind, Right Handed Aggressor: Rotate to your Right.

View from other side:

From Behind, Left Handed Aggressor: Rotate to your Right.

-

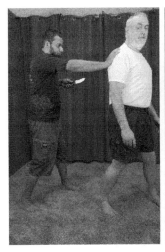 

View from other side and finish attacking the non-weapon arm quickly and with intent because you do not have control of the weapon arm:

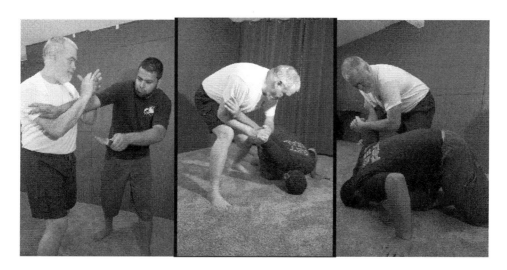

Assaults from behind are so surprising it is better to operant condition one single response to avoid delays therefore regardless of where the knife might be we rotate to our right.

**NOTE THE PRINCIPLES:** The principles here should be leaping out at you by now. You can see the rotation is possible no matter how the Aggressor grabs us because we do it through empty space. Once we have rotated all the notes from the side assassination attempts on principles apply here as well. I hope you can now see you stretch the aggressor out by moving to the empty space at the point where they have no contact with the ground. I hope you can see how we bone slave the arm to us so when we move our skeletal structure theirs moves too. I hope you can see how we tap into that free force of gravity to add our mass driving them into the ground. I am sure by now you can see all the principles that are underneath our techniques making them work.

# What if I can't tell which hand has the knife?

**This is a vital piece of information for your operant conditioning.** One of the things we've found when pressing the assassination attacks from the front in the "eyes closed" operant conditioning drills to simulate being taken by surprise, is that it can be hard to determine immediately which hand the knife is in and respond moving to the outside of the weapon arm. This creates a delayed response that could be fatal. We have a conditioned response for being surprised from the side and from behind but what about from the front when there is no indication which hand has the knife or there was going to be an attack? What do we do?

We have just learned that when the assassination is from the side we go to the side we are being attacked from regardless of which hand has the knife. We can apply a similar thought process here. If surprised rotate to the outside of the arm closest to you.

If that is the weapon arm, bonus. If not go to control the non-weapon arm and even if the arm is bent you will distance yourself from the weapon arm and to get to you they must shift and because your rotation created distance their movements become bigger and you respond accordingly now knowing where the knife is.

If you are struggling in the operant conditioning drills try this method of rotating to the outside of the arm closest to you to create distance to create time to see.

# Operant Conditioning Drill #12:

You will have noticed we've done assassination attempts from both sides and now from behind without a conditioning drill yet. That is deliberate. We now want to condition our response to a total surprise attack from any side. Hopefully that contact is a touch or indexing but even if it is a stab we need to respond and rotate immediately. Remember we have the response to rotate to the side we are contacted on, we rotate to the right if contacted from behind (or left if you prefer) and when surprised from the front and don't know where the knife is we go for the outside of the nearest arm.

The Drill:

The Respondent closes their eyes and the Aggressor can walk around and attack from any side. The Aggressor can begin slow but if working with a soft safe training knife you can work up to full speed and intent.

We have dealt with all kinds of the Aggressor assaulting us and getting close to us, but in all cases, we have been able to intercept. Now we will deal with being caught off guard and the Aggressor wants something from us either our stuff (Resource Predator) or us or someone with us (Process Predator).

# Situations

In these situations, you have been taken by surprise and the knife is pressed against you. Luckily for you the Aggressor has decided for that moment not to kill you. At this time, you may be able to talk your way out of the situation or, as can happen in a sexual assault, wait until the knife is removed from your body before acting.

If you think over how and when you might be facing an Aggressor with a knife this may be your likelihood. If sexual assault is a potential threat then being intimidated into compliance with a knife is a possibility.

However, this may only be a means to control you as others hurt your family, or you may believe you will be killed later.

It may be the means by which they get your compliance to go to "The Second Crime Scene".

# THE SECOND CRIME SCENE

Very often police refer to the "second crime scene". This is where a person has been taken from one area (the first crime scene) to another area where the assault takes place.

The location where the actual assault takes place is the second crime scene. The perpetrator must get you to the second crime scene because he does not believe he can commit the assault in the first location. This is often because the first location does not give them the Privacy and Control they need.

Whenever possible DO NOT GO TO THE SECOND CRIME SCENE, FIGHT BACK FIRST.

**YOUR ADVANTAGE**

When held at knifepoint, for the moment the Aggressor is not attacking therefore the advantage is yours. Yes, you have the advantage. You get to move first and they have to react to you.

When someone is in front of you with a knife, you have to **see** them move, **analyse** the attack, and **react** to it, which is why we work to build a tactical habit. The Aggressor just has to **move**. You have to do three things to their one. They have the advantage. (What saves you is the distance they have to go to get to you.) But when the knife is at your throat, and they are not just slicing it, then you **move**. They must **see**, **analyse**, and **react**. You have the three to one advantage. This is why we work so hard on making every response the same so that decisions are limited.

Situations where the Aggressor has the knife to your throat from behind follow the same tactics, but the expression is different than we have seen so far; therefore, they will be dealt with last. The three tactics of knife defence are still applicable. They may be modified slightly because of the close proximity to the Aggressor and how the knife is positioned on your body.

When you find yourself in a situation we want to add another advantage by getting our hands into a position to best execute a CBI. When a person puts a knife on you it is to intimidate; therefore, a submissive move may go without alarm. For example, the knife pointed to your midsection, we raise our hands BUT NOT

UP ALL THE WAY UP IN SURRENDER, but in what looks like giving up but is in fact moving them closer to where we need them.

However, you need to practice this so it looks innocent and doesn't look like you are about to pounce.

Another tactic is to ask a question, any question, right before you move. This can distract and shift their thinking and delay their reactions.

# SITUATIONS HANDLED AS WE HAVE THE OTHER ASSAULTS

There is often a simple way to incorporate the defence set out as our standard defence if you just look for the similarities. Try out different situations: knife to your lower back, knife to your side, and so on. Find a defence by following the principles:

1. **Avoid while intercepting the attack:** Hip Rotation to move away from the blade's attack and get an arm (upper or lower depends on height the blade is held at) between it.
2. **Control Lunge Step and Take Control of the Weapon Arm:** The rotation and intercept will place you in the usual position often to take control of the weapon arm and lunge step and lunge step to rip their structure from them.

**Stop the Threat**

- Once off balance, finish according to appropriate responses.

Approach training and practicing situations as a problem-solving exercise. They are a way to train you to see where the blade may go, how you need to rotate to avoid that attack, how you can get your arms on the weapon arm and how you might finish.

**NOTE ON AVOID THE ATTACK:** The knife against your body has a logical direction to assault you. Point against your body will be a thrust. Edge against your body will be a cut and the direction of the cut should be logical to the way the knife is held. Therefore, your movement to avoid should take you off that logical line of attack, not into it.

**Example #1**

The Aggressor is to your left side with the knife pointed into your ribs (right handed).

Because of the positioning of the knife on our body we can respond just as we did with an assassination attempt from our right side:

1) **Avoid while intercepting the attack:** Hip rotation to your right to move away from the direction the knife would attack. Use your right arm (rear arm of CBI) to intercept the Aggressor's weapon arm and direct it away from you.

2) **Control Lunge Step and take control of the weapon arm:** You can now finish with a Step Through Hip Rotation with left leg driving into their arm as you shear through and take.

3) **Stop the threat:** Once off balance, finish according to appropriate responses.

In the pictures below look how my right arm intercepts and guides the weapon arm away and as I continue to rotate it my left arm engages the weapon arm and I am now rotated off the line of attack and in the CBI position.

However, in situations where the knife is located makes a difference as to how you move.

Look at the pictures below. This seems like the same situation as previously with the Aggressor and knife on our right side, but this time the knife is held more on my stomach making a right rotation into the expected stab. This time I slide forward with a left rotation slipping the rear hand of the CBI in to deflect the knife away and prevent the stab:

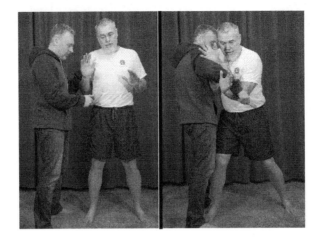

Once the CBI is in place I slide in a little deeper and slip the Clamp on then slide back applying the clamp to stretch the Aggressor off their base and to the ground:

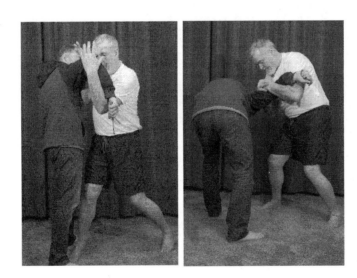

**NOTE THE PRINCIPLES:** All out principles stay with us. We rotate to open some empty space to slide our CBI into place. We move with our centre to drive their elbow up into empty space. We apply the Clamp locking their bones to ours (Bone Slaving). We rotate and sink onto the weapon arm using gravity to either break it or step back to drive them to the ground. Note again when taking them to the ground we stretch them over the weapon arm "corner" of the body because we have control and it cannot touch the ground to give their balance back.

**Example #2**

The Aggressor is in front with knife pointed to your mid-section (right handed).

1) **Avoid while intercepting the attack:** Hip rotation to your left to move away from the direction the knife would attack. Use your left arm (rear of CBI) to intercept the Aggressor's weapon arm away from you

2) **Control Lunge Step and take control of the weapon arm:** As you take control of the weapon arm use the Caesar move (see reversals) to rotate right and Clamp the weapon arm for a takedown.

3) **Stop the threat:** Once off balance, finish according to appropriate responses.

A left or right rotation will depend on where the knife is on your body. In the pictures below the knife is left of my centre line suggesting a left rotation. Right of the centre line a right rotation.

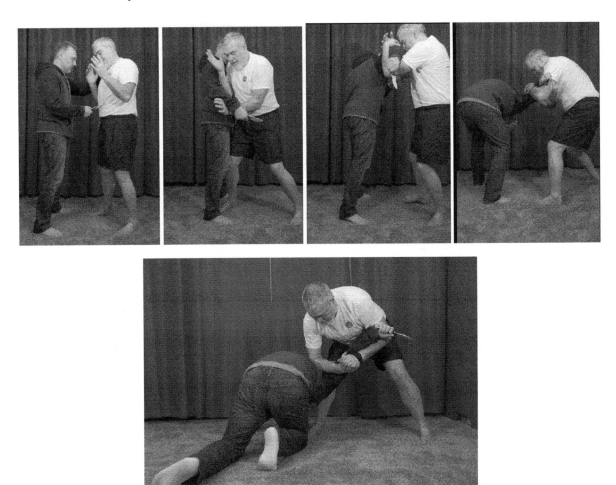

**NOTE THE PRINCIPLES:** All the same principles applied in the above examples as were applied in Example #1. Can you see them?

**Example #3**

The Aggressor is behind you with the knife held point into your back (the odds say it will be right handed but with how we move it really doesn't matter which hand the knife is in), therefore, we handle this just as we did the assassination attempt from behind rotating to the right always.

1) **Avoid while intercepting the attack:** Hip Rotation to your right to move away from the direction the knife would attack. Swing your right arm (rear of CBI) to intercept the Aggressor's weapon arm away from you. Keep your left arm high.

2) **Controlled Lunge Step and take control of the weapon arm:**

Right Hand Aggressor: Use a Step Through Hip Rotation with your left foot to drive them face first as you take control of the weapon arm with your right hand (front arm of CBI) or reverse directions and use the clamp to take them down.

Left Hand Aggressor: Overlap your hands on the back of their elbow, rotate left AS you step back to straight arm bar the weapon arm and drive them over.

3) **Stop the threat:** Once off balance, finish according to appropriate responses.

Here we choose a right rotation simply because the odds are the Aggressor is right handed and a right rotation places us outside the weapon arm.

However, it doesn't matter if the knife is in their left or right hand you rotate and CBI the same, then you take control of the weapon arm.

Right Hand:

**NOTE THE PRINCIPLES:** We rotate into and through empty space to change the direction we are facing. We STICK immediately to the weapon arm.

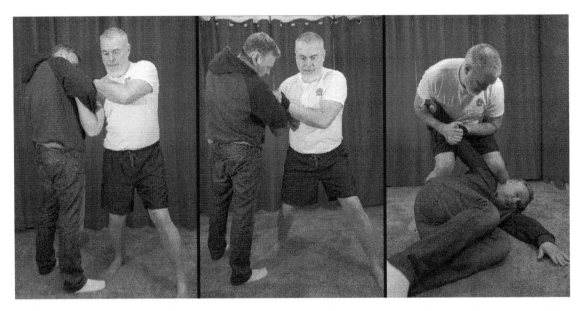

**NOTE THE PRINCIPLES:** We stick to the weapon arm (bone slaving) and immediately rotated back taking their elbow out of structure and into empty space. We step back into a longer stance so we can drop our centre sinking onto the weapon arm's elbow (gravity is always there for you.) Because the Aggressor's elbow is off their base dropping our weight/mass onto it drops the Aggressor into the ground. You must have the elbow away from the Aggressor's body or the tendency is try and drop it down and through their structure rather than empty space and that simply does not work.

Left Hand:

**NOTE THE PRINCIPLES:** Did you see what was used to get to safely face the Aggressor? Did you see what was used to stretch the Aggressor's weapon arm out? Did you what was used to control or break the weapon arm?

**Example #4**

Aggressor in front of you holding your lapel while placing the knife up under your throat.

In these cases, we often need our hands closer to the knife (say at our throat), but reaching may get us killed. So calmly, slowly, raise your hands as if surrendering, but don't hold your arms out from your body in the "hands up" position. Instead, keep them closer and thus closer to the weapon arm.

1) **Avoid while intercepting the attack:** Hip Rotation to your right, making sure your head and neck pull back off the line of force. You are going to perform a small the CBI almost with the wrists as you rotate, but as you do you can bring your left elbow in line with theirs taking that control point. Easily transitions into The Clamp.

2) **Control Lunge Step and Take control of the weapon arm.**

3) **Stop the threat:** Once off balance, finish according to appropriate responses.

**NOTE THE PRINCIPLES:** Notice how quickly the rotation put us in position to lock on and use Bone Slaving to manipulate the Aggressor.

As you can see, the steps in most situations do not change when the knife is already on you, but this time, because they have not carried through, the lack of distance is in your favour.

## Additional Drills

Work the same positions, but with the Aggressor on your left side, using different positions on your arm.

Work all sides, with the Aggressor controlling with the non-weapon arm.

Work left handed assaults.

Keep it real. Do not, as Rory Miller would call it, "In Breed" just to make things hard. Keep the situations ones that would happen, not a triple twist of your wrist to cover the blade or so on.

# SITUATIONS WHERE THE TACTICS REMAIN BUT THE TECHNIQUES ALTER

AGAIN: In these cases, we often need our hands closer to the knife (say at our throat), but reaching may get us killed. So calmly, slowly, raise your hands as if surrendering, but don't hold your arms out from your body in the "hands up" position. Instead, keep them closer and thus closer to the weapon arm.

### Aggressor Behind You with the Knife to Your Throat

### Alternative A

1) **Avoid the attack:** You must clear your neck away from the knife. To do this you take a very small step out to the side with your right foot, then twist your head left while simultaneously dropping downward. You press the back of your head into the crux of the Aggressor's elbow. Press your chin down. This briefly creates a space between your neck and the blade.

   **Intercept the attack:** At the same time, bring your hands up to grip the weapon hand. Your left hand (high hand of CBI) comes up inside between your throat and the weapon hand if possible. Your right hand grasps the weapon hand. Grab firmly. (Your left hand may end up grabbing the blade. While this is not recommended, it is better than a slit throat. If you do grab the blade, try to pinch the blade between your fingers.)

**Take control of the weapon arm:** You must grab the weapon hand (if you grab the wrist the Aggressor will have too much movement possible with the blade and could cut you badly), then immediately take a Control Lunge Step controlled lunge step back ducking under the weapon arm to place them in a straight arm bar position controlled lunge step back ducking under the weapon arm to place them in an arm bar position.

Another option is to twist the Aggressor's hand out as you step forward and out of the hold. Turn Back to your right, towards the Aggressor and strike.

2) **Stop the threat:** Continue applying the twist on the Aggressor's wrist as you twist to your right. If done at full speed the Aggressor will be taken down and in a position to leave and escape, distance and deploy, disable or control.

**NOTE THE PRINCIPLES:** We can move our throat away from the knife because there is empty space between the back of our head and the crux of the Aggressor's elbow. We take control of the weapon arm by grabbing. People tell me I have a grip that is hard to get away from and I believe the reason is what might be called micro bone slaving. When I grab I picture my bones fusing to their bones, so when I move my hands whatever I have a hold of is part of me and moves too.

**Alternative B**

1) **Avoid the attack:** With your right hand, reach up and strike with your palm on the Aggressor's right elbow driving the elbow (arm) to your left. Simultaneously, turn your head to your right and press your chin into the crux of the Aggressor's elbow. (This takes your neck away from the blade.)

   **Intercept the attack and take control of the weapon arm:** At the same time, grip tightly with your left hand to hold the weapon arm in position and pull the Aggressor's elbow towards you as you step back with your right foot pulling the elbow out from underneath.

2) **Control Lunge Step:** Continue pulling the elbow out from under as you now drive the arm over the top. This will lock the elbow and take the Aggressor down. Step backwards deeply.

3) **Stop the threat:** You have taken their balance and now they can be propelled or taken down. More twisting of the arm could damage the shoulder to disable.

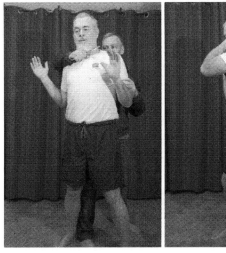

**NOTE THE PRINCIPLES:** Can you see the rotation to empty space? Can you see the bone slaving?

> **Teaching Notes:**
>
> One of the reasons I wanted to include these last two approaches for a knife held to your throat was to show that although the "technique" looked different from those we've been using the tactics, and the underlying principles that made them work remained the same.
>
> While situations are very possible (particularly for women and others susceptible to sexual assault) I like working them because of the problem-solving aspect that require you to think through where the knife is most likely going to go, where I should go to avoid, the best option to intercept and from there how should I finish. All these things are consistent with solving any knife assault.

That concludes dealing with an Aggressor up close and personal but we haven't dealt with one keeping their distance and Hacking at us.

# You've Propelled the Aggressor away – Now what?

One of our tactics is to propel the Aggressor away so that we can implement the strategy of escape. Once we have propelled the Aggressor away then the follow up is easy enough if we have scoped out an escape route which takes us to a safe populated place. One thing you can add to your escape, when possible, is deliberately bumping into cars as you run hoping to set off the alarms and draw attention.

Another strategy we have is to distance and deploy or obtain a weapon.

The first thing we will cover is having propelled the Aggressor away in hopes of deploying or grabbing a weapon but we haven't had time yet and now the Aggressor is closing but not close enough for us to intercept and they are hacking at our limbs.

# Defeating the HACK Without a Weapon

You have successfully distanced the Aggressor, but have not had time to deploy a weapon or grab an improvised weapon, now they are coming at you not with large movements, but with short, tight, quick movements attempting to hack at your hands and arms, never coming close enough for you to intercept, and without enough commitment or movement to clear the attack.

When you fight knife against knife, there is a method used in Filipino fighting called "defanging the snake". Every time the knife hand is in range, you strike it with your knife. While we do not have a blade, we do have two hands. You would use the same approach with an expandable baton vs. a knife.

- Form your hands into what Uechi Ryu calls Hiraken (Tiger Paws) or Front Knuckle Fists. This is done by forming partial fists so that the second set of knuckles is extended and used as the striking surface rather than the third larger set of knuckles usually used in striking with a fist. These are pointed knuckles that can be used to pin point strike or rip across the hands or top of the forearms. I call these your personal set of knives.

- The Respondent is in the described protective position (See How to stand when defending against a knife).
- As the Aggressor moves closer, snap a quickly retracted strike at the back of the hand or top or inner forearm (the back of the forearm is too tough to hurt).

The back of the hand is an excellent target, but be very careful when training and **use pads**. There are many small bones in the back of the hand and they break easy.

This can induce pain and may give you an opportunity to proceed.

Pain may not deter the attacker, but you may damage their hands enough to decrease efficiency and you may beat their mind if they feel they have lost the advantage of surprise and the threat of a knife.

**NOTE THE PRINCIPLE:** The main principle here is to control the distance. We want to keep the Aggressor at a distance where they cannot put the knife into our body. We stay where we can attack their hand (yes, they can attack ours from here too so pay attention.)

## DRILL: Beat the Hack

**Safety Notes:** You need protective gloves such as hockey gloves to do this safely. Without them the Aggressor's hand can be broken.

Without protective gloves to wear when simply learning the concept, the Respondent can slap the back of the Aggressor's weapon hand to explore the timing, BUT this should not be how it is practiced or you will habituate a slap rather than the proper knuckle strike.

- The Aggressor takes the knife in a protected hand.
- The Aggressor stands about "sparring" distance from the Respondent as if they have broken contact.
- The Aggressor uses short "hacking" and quick motions to cut the Respondent's hands, arms etc., to distract and wear down so they can close and attack.
- The focus for the DRILL is on the quick hacking attacks.
- The Respondent uses the Front Knuckle Fists and times their attacks to the back to the Aggressor's hands.
- Go for it and have fun.

## Using a Baton and Improvised Weapons

We have propelled the Aggressor away and we have had time to either deploy a baton or grab an improvised weapon. Now we will look at how to use them to defend yourself and defeat the Hack.

The use of a baton for Law Enforcement or Security is covered under the Long Rigid Weapons section.

As stated previously, whenever possible do not go empty hand vs. a knife. Try to arm yourself.

Any stick, cane, umbrella, long flashlight, tennis (or handball or squash) racquet, an antenna off an old car, a snow scraper, a heavy jacket, a belt, a purse, or a backpack will do. Or if you are in law enforcement or security a baton will be used as described in the Long Rigid Weapons section below.

Weapons fall into distinct categories and need to be applied based on their characteristics.

# In all cases of using a weapon you take Control of the Distance.

**NOTE:** I will not address the issue of firearms, as I am not qualified to do so. While I did carry a firearm to protect money, often a lot of money, as an armed guard the job completely different than law enforcement. For those in law enforcement who may carry for a variety of reasons, your Departmental policies on the use of firearms would override anything I might have presented, anyway.

# Long Rigid Weapons

Baton (usually not an improvised weapon but it will reinforce the use to most), stick, long flashlight, tennis (or handball or squash) racquet, an antenna off a car, a snow scraper, anything that has some length to it and will not bend (or hopefully break).

## Application: Distance and hit the weapon hand

- Keep moving back.
- Use short quick strikes to attack the weapon hand.
- **DO NOT** use big movements because it is too easy to miss and carry through opening yourself to attack. Think of your body like a cookie cutter and you must remain inside the outside of the cookie cutter = your body's outline.
- Do not try to strike to the Aggressor's body with the weapon until they have dropped the knife.

In Filipino fighting this is often called "defanging the snake".

This is the same approach we took with our "personal set of knives" (fore knuckles.)

**NOTE THE PRINCIPLES:** Look at the use of the stick above. The strikes are done with a rotation of the body. The arms are moved, they are not moving. Because of this you can control the weapon and not over extend any strike. Also note the rotation of the wrist as the stick strikes.

## Flexible Weapons

A heavy jacket, a belt, a purse, booster cables, bungie cord, rope or a backpack will do.

Application: DISTANCE AND SWING ALTERNATING TO THE EYES AND WEAPON HAND

- It should be held with the first three fingers of one hand pinning them with the thumb and fourth finger (as you would hold the reins of a horse).

    For example, you would hold a coat at the collar, a purse by the strap, back pack, belt, rope etc.

- Swing the flexible weapon in a figure eight pattern alternating from attacking the weapon hand and swinging at the Aggressor's eyes.

- You can shorten the arc by using your free hand part way along the weapon to effectively shorten the weapon itself.
- The Aggressor may grab this weapon with their free hand. If this happens immediately attack their legs with a kick.
- Again no large movements that take you into a wide swing leaving an opening for the Aggressor to step in and strike.

For flexible weapons you also work the principles: **DISTANCE AND HIT THE WEAPON HAND, HIT THE EYES**.

**NOTE THE PRINCIPLES:** Can you see the strike was done with a rotation and the arms were moved (note how the arms are still well aligned for structure?)

## Short Rigid Weapons

Pen, comb, key, pocket stick or similar tool.

Application: DISTANCE AND HIT THE WEAPON HAND

- Keep moving back.
- Use short quick strikes to attack the weapon hand.
- Do not use big movements because it is too easy to miss and carry through opening yourself to attack.
- Do not try to strike the Aggressor's body with the weapon until they have dropped the knife.

## Additional Weapons of Opportunity

Anything that you can distract the Aggressor with can help your defence.

Loose change, keys, or even bills thrown in the Aggressor's face may give you a moment to escape.

I've seen a video clip where the person threw a baseball cap striking the Aggressor with the rigid brow.

A chair or stool can place a strong object between you and the Aggressor and the legs can be used to stab at them with.

Be creative.

As stated it is always better to grab something to protect yourself with. This is because most weapons increase the distance between you and the knife. The Psychology of the fight changes. Rory Miller says most people quit in their minds before their bodies. Hit a person real hard with a tennis racquet in the hand or swing a heavy belt buckle past their eyes and see if they want to swing the knife at you again. That is assuming they are still holding the knife. Anything is better than nothing.

## Okay Now Let's Get Real

But before we get to that I want you to consider an old martial art saying: "You must have form without form." YES, like all old martial arts sayings at first it sounds like BS from a movie but once you get what it means it makes all the sense in the world. In this manual, I have given you a form, a technique, a structure or approach to increasing your options for survival against a knife. What underlies that "form" are the tactics and principles to make it work. That is the true form. If what you do follows the tactics and the principles and IT WORKS then it doesn't have to look like the pictures in this manual. You will have the form without form. You have had the training so now comes the practice where FUNCTION is more important than FORM.

So now let's get real, knife assaults are fast, vicious and almost always the element of surprise is used by the Aggressor.

What this means is you will find yourself in the centre of a deadly hurricane of chaotic violence. The framework given to you in this manual is so that your mind has a vision and idea of what is needed to be done. What that vision looks like in the end is immaterial as long as it works.

To try and memorize how to respond to a knife assault when you have no idea of how the blade is going to come until the Aggressor moves is never ever going to look like the Training.

I am not saying you won't do what you trained I am saying it may not look like it did in training and it doesn't have to.

What do you need?

Find the eye of the hurricane with the principles.

Avoid while intercepting: Get your ass off the line of attack and place a decent structure onto the weapon arm.

What next?

Use that structure to control the Aggressor either to propel away or to lock on.

Then end the threat.

You know how to think ahead and make decisions now on how to get to your goal to survive.

You now have trained to get a sense of how a blade moves once it starts.

You now know how to rotate to avoid that blade.

You know how to intercept and attach your sensors to that weapon arm.

You know where the control point on the weapon arm is and that your goal is command over that point.

You know how to use that contact through shearing and leverage to manipulate that Aggressor.

You know to use the empty space to avoid the Aggressor's strength.

You know how to survive.

Everything is there.

The techniques are provided as a guide, a path to success.

The techniques are there to illustrate the principles and what is needed to survive.

Once you have trained, worked through the drills, experienced the techniques, worked the tactical sensitivity drill and the hand drill enough that you can get a read on that knife's path, then all that remains is to play.

Yes, the next step is to play and explore and find what works and how far you can push.

What you will find is when it fails it fails not so much because you didn't do precisely the move but rather you left out a principle. You didn't rotate; therefore, you fought to block the attack rather than avoid, you weren't facing empty space so you tried out muscle the Aggressor through their structure.

When you tried to manipulate the Aggressor did you shear? Did you have the control point? Were you working to move you?

You will quickly find the best grip means nothing if you're trying to fight.

Don't look for a fight look to survive.

Be creative and come up with your own but for now play with these.

I recommend using a safe training blade for these drills so your partner can scale up their resistance to end at full out trying to kill you.

The next drills are just out and out creative play. Work everything. Come up with your own as well.

# Drills:

### Skill Set Play:

The danger in these is doing them so much you forget they are only to gain a skill set and begin to think they are knife defence.

### Pass it By:

Purpose: Sometimes just getting your hands on the weapon arm enough to not get stabbed by the initial surprise attack is enough to give you the opportunity to survive.

Start in the middle of a room and have the Aggressor slash and stab and you just pass it by but at some point, go for control or propel. You can PLAY and pass as many by as you think you can before going for the end.

Move the Respondent so their back is to a wall and repeat.

Move the Respondent so there are in a corner and repeat.

Repeat the whole drill this time pass it by as few times as possible before being in position to end.

### Control That:

Purpose: Understanding you need to end the threat as quickly as possible is important and failure is a great teacher.

Same approach as above but this time take control of the weapon arm and try to keep control as long as you can without finishing.

The Aggressor should work at getting free, using the non-weapon hand, even changing the weapon hand to kill you.

**Operant Conditioning Play:**

The purpose is to take all the skills and training and push the boundaries.

I am not going to say it is okay to die in this training but if your partner hasn't killed you a few times every night – get a more skilled partner.

Even though your partner is going to try and kill you this still isn't a competition, and by that, I mean "keep it real." Don't add in BS just to stab your partner because you know what they are going to do.

Your job is to make them better so push their boundaries.

**Interview:**

Aggressor comes to your side and attacks.

If they are going to attack from behind have them index (touch, grab with the non-weapon arm) just before the strike.

If you get good at this try having them initiate a conversation with you before attacking.

If you get good at this try walking and focus on counting backwards from ten.

**Survival Note:** NOTHING says you have to stay in an uncomfortable range. If they "appear" at your shoulder and begin to talk give yourself permission to AVOID by getting back to a comfortable distance.

**Assassination:**

Walk from one end of a room to the other and have one or more partners walk towards you.

When the Aggressor gets close they attack from your side.

If the Aggressor is going to wait until passed you they should index, there is no "Spider Sense" I can give you for the sociopath just walking by and reverse grip stabs you as they pass and keep going.

If you get good at this try walking and focus on counting backwards from ten.

**Scenario:**

Design your own but ATM, parkade, washroom – decide if it is an outright assault a knife on the body to get control through intimidation.

**That Went Bad:**

Do any drill that involves an empty hand assault but at some point, the Aggressor draws a (training) blade either theirs or the Respondent's depending on how you set it up.

If you happen to carry a cutting tool (a knife) then get a good training replica and have it on you, so it can be accessed by the Aggressor.

Think over your life or your job and where you are most likely to encounter a knife and how.

- Simply set up that situation and begin slowly, then add speed so you move from soft adrenaline practice to hard adrenaline practice.

# Redo all the attacks from various angles.

# Have your partner do a variety of attacks one after the other resetting as quickly as possible

# Have a partner take a soft training knife and from up close try to kill you with it – pick up speed and intensity but be careful not to break your partner's arm.

**MOST IMPORTANTLY PLAY AND HAVE FUN.**

---

**Safety Note:** Always ALWAYS make sure you don't have a live blade. So if for any reason you have a trainer and take a break (lunch), when returning to training always pat yourself down and make sure you have replaced live blades with a SAFE trainer.
**Final Safety Note:** PROTECT YOUR EYES!

# Trouble Shooting

So, practice isn't going well. You keep getting killed or you are unable to control that weapon arm.

What's wrong?

Here's the thing, if the principles are followed things will work. When things aren't working look at whether you've hit the principles.

Did you rotate to 90 degrees to the weapon arm or are you facing into the Aggressor's structure?

Not rotating enough leads to failure.

When you moved did you move into empty space or into their structure (trying to out muscle them)?

Not using empty space leads to failure.

When you took control of the weapon arm did you pull it to you or did you move to the weapon arm?

Pulling the arm to you worsens your position and leads to failure.

When you moved have you slaved their bones to yours?

Bone slaving allows you to move them as you move, not doing this leads to failure.

When you wanted to drive them into the ground did you use empty space and gravity or did you try to muscle them over?

Use gravity it is free and powerful not using gravity can lead to failure.

Pretty much run through the principles and see what is missing to discover why things failed.

# Conclusion

We've reached the end of the book. Well, except for the addendums, please read them as well.

I hope certain principles from this book forever stand out in your mind, because they will not only enable and enhance your knife defence but any application of force:

- Move YOU not THEM.
- Empty Space.
- Rotation.
- Structure.
- Arms are MOVED not Moving.
- Loose.
- Tendon Power.
- Leverage.
- Shearing.
- Control the Distance.
- Balance.
- Move with your Centre.
- Gravity.
- Bone Slaving.
- Swallow.
- Smother.
- Wringing out the towel.
- Elasticity.
- Act in Motion.
- Sticking, Adhering, Guiding and Leading.
- Never Alarm the Aggressor.

As you work through the progression set out as the attacks shrink your responses will shrink, and once you've shrunk your moves in response you may well find your movements stay small no matter the distance the Aggressor is coming from and as long as you continue to rotate that 90 degrees to the weapon arm, small movements are just fine. However, the large CBI is excellent when rotating off contact and not knowing where the knife is.

You should focus on your chosen Tactics set more than the other, but still work both. You should work the slow training until the techniques are habituated and then work them hard against more resistance.

Work through play and build an enjoyment into the success of the moves, as this will enhance the operant conditioning.

It should be clear that this approach has made the responses as similar as possible. You rotate and intercept. You want the outside of the weapon arm but the inside works too. Left hand or right hand makes little difference beyond a different visual. The only difference that requires drilling is the front hand of the CBI is high and the rear low and THAT does change depending on which way you rotate. Front hand up, rear hand down simply gives you more options. However, through drilling this become second nature. We want as few decisions to make as possible.

## FINAL SURVIVAL HINTS:

- When things are not working never be reluctant to propel the Aggressor away and either escape, grab/deploy a weapon or simply distance and reset.
- When moving one way if you are not gaining control (person resets their balance quickly) reverse directions and take them the other way – repeat switching directions until they cannot resist.
- Control is the hardest option so always remember you can shift to disable to remain safe and finish or to disrupt the Aggressor so that you can take control.

My goal is to make people safer so I hope this manual helps in at least some small way. There are no guarantees in empty hand vs. knife, we can only hope to increase our chances of survival.

If you want more fun just play and see how well this foundation works on non-knife attacks (but that is for another book.)

Speaking of another book watch for my next book: "From the Ground Up: Counter Assault Ground Fighting." Visit the WPD-RC website to join the notification list: http://wpd-rc.com/book-list/

If you found this book enjoyable or helpful I hope you will consider writing a short review on Amazon. Reviews help small publications such as this to get noticed.

Check out my website and Facebook pages:

wpd-rc.com

# Addendum #1: Operant Conditioning to Habit Response

"We don't rise to the level of our expectations — we fall to the level of our training." — Archilochus a Greek soldier.

Simply put, operant conditioning is a behaviour modification method where certain responses to stimuli are either rewarded if the response is the desired one or punished if it is not. A Habit is a deeply imprinted response to a cue. We want to use operant conditioning to create a habit response to specific cue.

**What do we want?**

Reacting is usually described as working on the OODA system:

1. **Observe** what is happening.
2. **Orient** to the observation (interpret the sensory input).
3. **Decide** what to do about it.
4. **Act**.

The delays in reacting come when:

1. You freeze at observe or orient or decide.
2. There are too many options to decide what to do.

But what if we could act directly off the observation, basically short circuiting OODA and leaping from Observe to Act?

This is where HABITS come in.

**Habit is a three step process**

1. The Cue: the stimulus that kicks off the accessing of this habit.
2. The Routine: the programmed response.
3. The Reward: why the brain kept this response.

Habits work in the Basal Ganglia of the brain and once a habit is formed the rest of the brain basically bows out when the cue is seen and lets the Basal Ganglia take over. In fact, once a habit kicks in the rest of the brain cannot interfere.

Remember we want to jump from Observe (the **Cue**) to Act (the **Routine**).

The formation of a habit means once the cue is noted (OBSERVED) you enter immediately into the routine (ACT).

Therefore, if we can form the right habits we can respond faster than normal by jumping from Observe to Act.

Habits CAN be created.

Habits CAN be changed.

**IF** we can break the habit down we can create, change, or even eliminate it.

# THE SYSTEM

### Operant Conditioning:

### Forming Tactical Habits

My system works on forming effective combative HABITS through Detailed Analysis of the Cue and Reward, Operant Conditioning and Soft Adrenaline Training.

### Detailed Analysis of Cue and Reward

To create a habit, you must:

1. Identify the cue.
2. Identify the "True" reward.
3. Determine the Routine.
4. Believe it works.

To CHANGE a habit, you must:

1. Keep the cue the same.
2. Identify and keep the "True" reward the same.
3. Change the Routine.
4. Believe it works.

## Identification of "Cues" to Create a Habit

The cue is the time you need to move and act, or as Rory Miller says that moment people need to have "permission" to act and the cue builds in that permission. My good friend and training partner, Laird Elliot calls it setting the Trigger.

One step is to review who you are, what you do, and what dangers you may face.

The next step is to run through those danger situations in detail to identifying what the first indication of danger is and how to act, and also the last indication and how to act (you know, for when Mr. Murphy jumps in).

**NOTE:** This will take studying violence as opposed to assuming how it will happen, or how you think it will happen. Unless you have experienced it or done it, you must study it. So much of what people think violence is comes from mass media (TV or movies) or a limited personal experience.

This includes analysis of assault movement and precursors. WHAT DO YOU SEE?

This includes scenario visualization, dissection and analysis, and making decisions on what or can or are willing to do. (Do your thinking now, not later.)

What do you see leads to the earliest "Cue".

Here is an example of identifying a cue. I was training a personal protection specialist responsible for protecting a high-level politician. This was a very experienced man and he and his team could identify a threat and act but he had one puzzle he was trying to solve.

Politicians and public figures are open to violent assault but they are also subject to a humiliating assault. There had been a trend of people hitting public figures in the face with pies. A great joke for the perpetrator but humiliating to the politician and it opened questions about their protection team.

The puzzle he faced was that people with violent intent tended to move a certain way and have certain facial expressions. These were cues he could identify and move in on what could be a threat.

The people using pies thought it was a joke so they did not give off these cues.

In talking things over and watching videos I determined the one common factor was that the pie (or weapon) had to remain out of sight. Just like the possibility of a knife being there when you cannot see the hands, a pie could be there.

So, the cue of someone approaching the politician with a hidden hand was added to what he would watch for.

The cue would be a hidden hand and then a response was needed.

The response was also a problem because you cannot slam a person to the ground simply because you cannot see their hands. The person could be approaching the politician to deliver a letter or petition or simply have phone.

The response had to be able to determine what was in the hand without the action going viral on the net. And yes, I came up with a way to intercept and determine if the hand had a weapon, pie or nothing of danger but that solution is for my friend or perhaps a different book.

Identifying a cue for them to act on was the secret to preventing a humiliating assault. Clearly for this book the cue is the knife.

**Identification of Rewards**

You must identify and acknowledge what the reward is to establish or change the habit.

This means seeking and understanding what people are getting out of their current training.

Define winning an assault, for example. Is it looking the guy in the eyes so he knows he is beaten? Is it that feeling of physical clashing and manly conflict that makes it feels like winning? Or is an effortless win the true reward? If so, then this is the "feeling" we must seek and acknowledge as the true reward. One lady, and Alberta Peace Officer I was training at their 2017 annual conference dropped her partner (a strong man) and then in surprise said, "But I didn't do anything, I didn't feel anything." I smiled and told her that was how she knew she'd done it right.

This knife defence system takes an adjustment because it doesn't go force on force and clash, instead it works in the empty spaces and takes advantage of physics.

The required reward shift important to work through because people engage direct lines of force all the time because of the "manly reward" of that conflict. We must redefine the reward from manly conflict to survival and teach the habit of not engaging strength but engaging weakness.

Using Rory Miller's Goal = Strategy = Tactics = Techniques we can work at defining the Goal to survival and the have that reward to be properly acknowledged. We can go beyond the Monkey dance.

To be effective the reward has to be:

- immediate,
- consistent, and
- large enough to be valued.

## Instilling Belief

How do we instil belief?

By acknowledging that the failures feel bad and that successes feel good.

This is an ACTIVE acknowledgement.

In the next part we will look at Operant Conditioning and Soft Adrenaline Practice.

## Operant Conditioning

Operant conditioning (or instrumental conditioning) is a type of learning in which an individual's behaviour is modified by an immediate consequence. When the action is successful there is a positive reinforcement. When the action is unsuccessful there is a negative consequence. The goal is that the reinforcing of the successful behaviours embeds them as desirable ways to behave, where the negative consequences eliminates that behaviour.

Operant Conditioning is achieved through rewarding the desired behaviour and punishing the negative behaviour.

Habits are formed when the reward is achieved.

Therefore, habits can be formed through operant conditioning.

In our system, you are going to find something hard to accept for the first few repetitions in a drill where the participant is going to actively acknowledge that it either felt GREAT or it felt CRAPPY! Even if just to themselves.

This is an important piece for successful operant conditioning and absolutely necessary for the formation of a habit.

No corrections are made during Operant Conditioning.

It is important to not "jump in" as an instructor during operant conditioning. The teaching is done by success or failure. This is not the time to instruct. If the student cannot be successful, then break off from the Operant Conditioning Drills and return to teaching and training.

## Soft Adrenaline Practice

Soft Adrenaline Practice allows time for the success or failure of the routine to be experience and acknowledged, allowing the practitioner to retain the successes and eliminate the failures.

Therefore, Soft Adrenaline Practice allows Operant Conditioning to happen.

## Purpose

The first purpose of Soft Adrenaline Practice is to introduce a little of that KICK JUICE into your system while you are placed in a threatened environment. Anything that works for you here is recorded by your brain and body differently than something you learn "intellectually" and the brain and body recognize these as things to remember that are good for survival. People who drive and have successfully swerved around an object jumping in front of them know that action is embedded and easier next time.

Things you remember to do in response to something that your brain feels are important to remember are HABITS. Therefore, soft adrenaline practice is excellent for habit creation and habit change.

The other reason is that it allows us to find the best Routine or action as well. (No point conditioning if the routine is ineffective.)

I am only going to have one point on the routine itself which will follow the soft adrenaline description but the actual expression of the routine will be based in your own training and experience.

The purpose of slow training is to find what I am going to call the Pure Move.

The Pure Move is Rory Miller's Golden Move or my interpretation of it. The Pure Move is accomplished without attributes (i.e. speed, strength) and simultaneously achieves the following objectives: you avoid the assault, you achieve a strategic position, and you disrupt their structure (by control or strike).

## Why Eliminate Attributes in Practice?

My Soft Adrenaline preference is slow motion training is to eliminate any attributes you may have such as speed and strength.

If your success depends on an attribute, then your success is only good until you meet someone with more of those attributes.

Attributes are still used in application but they should only determine damage, not success.

In addition, we often cover our errors or flaws with an attribute. By this I mean if I can get from point A to Point C so fast the person does not see I didn't go through Point B as I should have then I was lucky. But if they do then they can take advantage. By going faster to cover my errors my training is flawed because the moment I encounter someone who can see the flaw who can take advantage of the flaw, I fail. Therefore, going slow allows me to see everything in between Point A and Point C and correct any flaws.

The Pure Move succeeds because the principles used are appropriate and appropriately applied to the situation.

Therefore, we want to eliminate the need of an attribute for success.

**Other Benefits of Slow Practice**

Here the other benefits of going slow enter into the picture: the ability to have a tactile experience of what you are doing.

Think of a small glass of something to drink (you pick the beverage). I take the glass and fire the liquid to the back of my throat and swallow.

Could I even begin to tell you what they liquid was, the consistency, what it tasted like, or even if I liked it?

If instead I took it and rolled it around in my mouth savouring the flavour and the consistence would I know more about that drink? If I enjoy the drink I will want to remember it to have again, but if I don't then I will also want to remember what it was so I can avoid it. Most people will express their like or dislike with either a facial expression or verbal comment or both. This is acknowledging the reward (or negative).

Slow training is intended to give you immediate feedback both positive and negative (the Operant Conditioning portion), because if I am making the wrong move and I do not cover it up with speed or strength then I should FEEL that I have lost my position, or my control, or my structure, or that smack upside my head. By going slow, I can savour the feeling of the move and embed within me what feels good and should be sought again and what feels bad and should be avoided.

Going slow also allows you to do complete movements. Going slow I can drive my elbow all the way through your jaw without injuring you as I would if it was fast (hence the flaw of pulling strikes when going fast in training – all training has some safety flaw.)

**Don't Exceed the "Fight" Threshold but Add Resistance**

The other thing that can be done in slow training is a progressive increase in resistance and fight of your partner.

But there is a "speed" that when reached will/should kick in your partner's fight response. Slow training should NEVER be done at that speed. Not only because it is not slow, but because we are trying to embed new tactical habits and kicking into fight mode will reinforce all old habits, inhibiting forming new and better ones.

We want our partner to provide a progressively level of resistance and IF we expect them to stay within the drill and go slowly and NOT kick into fight mode even when that speed is reached then we are embedding a failure and a bad one. Therefore, the speed that triggers the fight response has to be avoided at all costs or – accept your partner is no longer in the drill and should be fighting – which negates the purpose of a drill, so pause and start again.

Going slowly, your partner can begin to resist and fight back in a progressive manner teaching you where the holes in your fight are and teaching them to see the holes.

## Reading Lines of Incoming Force – The Ability to See

Going slowly allows you to see what I call the "flow." Now I am not talking about flowery frilly movements I am taking about lines of force and where they travel, where they might make you travel and how they can be influenced.

I'm talking about reading where and what will come based on the flow of the lines of force. Going slowly allows us to see things as they unfold, to read the attack.

If you can read the attack you can predict or influence where the holes will appear and be there. It is too late in the chaos to take advantage of an opening, you must go where the opening will be.

I remember years ago seeing a show on Wayne Gretzsky where his father talked about how when Wayne was a kid he would have him watch a hockey game with a drawing of the rink in front of him and a pencil. He would trace the path of the puck throughout the game and later study where the puck traveled so when he played he never chased the puck, he always just went to where the puck was going to be.

This is what slow motion can help you learn. Watch and see where not only things are but where they go and how the body reacts so that you can tell where the holes will appear and be there as they do.

## Body Awareness of Tactile Thinking

What I want here is a body awareness, a tactile "thinking" where what you feel is the cue to the next response.

Our body does not work by active thought. For instance, we do not think: "heart beat now", it beats on its own. We cannot think "he's slipping to the side so I have to move/slam/hit here." There cannot be an exchange of internal thoughts. Tactile thinking is body awareness and training a response to certain stimuli. The feeling is directly attached to your response, and your response will also be what HAS felt right (and worked) in practice.

This is one of the most important lessons and can only be learned by doing and experiencing.

Without feeling what is happening you will be far too late to respond successfully.

## Drills

In reality based training, the drills used are based off of the study of assaults not "fights." We have a number of drills, but if you can conceive of how a bad guy would try to take you out then you can create a drill to simulate it, then simply do it slowly.

## Hard Adrenaline Practice

Speed or Hard Adrenaline Practice can follow once the Routines are embedded.

Speed should never be introduced until the Routines are embedded.

It is not that you never practice with speed, but this slow practice specifically addresses using operant conditioning to create tactical habits. Adding speed will test how well they have been embedded.

## Final Notes

I know it is a long addendum but as a final note I have to repeat that in habit formation using operant conditioning there is no "training", no talking, no teaching, just the experience. What is felt, is the teacher.

This is what I call practice. Training is for teaching and corrections. Practice is for operant conditioning; the feedback is success or failure only. There are no corrections made during operant conditioning / practice. Absolutely no teaching (training) should go on during practice. However, if there is constant failure then STOP practicing and return to TRAINING, teaching what should be done.

# Addendum #2: Micro Moment Skill Set Progressive Training

## The Theory

Within every physical conflict there are micro moments when a particular skill set is required to either survive or capitalize on that moment.

Micro Moment Skill Set Progressive Training takes each of these required skill sets out of that moment and focuses on them, stretching that moment of time out, extending it, allowing them to be fully explored. You train them from this expanded and often simplified way back into the micro moment.

By doing this, we then have that skill set on call for that micro moment in which it is needed.

## The Background

In my base system, the common approach to teaching the skills required is through pre-set fighting sequences. These sequences are to transmit to the student all the skill sets required in a conflict.

My theory as to why this can't happen for some of the skills is that the skill sets demonstrated in those sets appear like the flash on a camera. FLASH they appear and disappear. This is a consistent factor in most drills regardless of their source.

The student gets to train that skill set only for that brief flash, in that particular context, as is the case in many drills be they Traditional Martial Arts or a Reality based System.

The limited exposure, the specific context, and the cooperative partner limit the ability to incorporate this skill set in a chaotic moment.

To address this issue, I decided to alter the manner in which the skill sets were transmitted.

We need to segregate the skill set out from the micro moment and expand the exposure time. To do this, we begin by solely using one main skill set. We then limit the input from our partner.

As we move through the progression of the drill, the exposure to the skill set shrinks back to that micro moment (think of a pyramid).

As we move through the progression of the drill, the action we apply it to begins to add in other elements therefore it broadens what is thrown at us (think of moving down the pyramid).

As the drill progresses, the partner (meat puppet) becomes less and less cooperative until they are fighting back at an appropriate level for the other student. (With glimpses of where the skill will go to as they advance.)

Now before I go any further, let me say that if these skill sets are not integrated back into the whole then they are useless to you. So, while I see segregating skill sets to be focused and developed, they must be brought back into the whole Martial Artist.

For instance, the Foundation Conditioning Drills from the Martial Arts school I ran are a skill set segregated. An over view would seem like the skill being trained were striking with power (actually hitting people) and taking a hit. On a closer look the skill being taught was to hit back immediately when struck.

Striking hard is a primary skill but a skill set that may be needed for a micro moment of a fight is to hit back immediately when struck.

The Tactile Sensitivity Drill and the Hand drill are micro moment skill set drills.

## Skill Set: Controlling the Distance

Now I see this skill set slightly differently than others and I really have nothing else to call it at the moment, so this is the term I am going to use. To me controlling the distance is that awareness as to where the opponent is and the ability to be not there when they try to strike you. This is often done with the most minimal of margins.

I see controlling the distance as a true micro moment skill set. A fight cannot be won by controlling the distance it can only be won by closing. However, when that Aggressor is just a little quicker than you expected or you get enough of a glimpse of the ambush to change it from total surprise to reaction, then controlling the distance in that micro moment of surprise is what may just get you to the next micro moment where you must close.

## Skill Set: Sticking Hands

I have always worked on Uechi versions of this drill, though as usual, we have taken it our own direction. In a real chaotic fight with fists flying there will not be the lovely control that a sticking hand drill demonstrates. However, for a micro moment you will need the sticking hands skill set to take control of the incoming energy and take command of that energy redirection and shutting down the Aggressor's attack. In knife defence we use sticking from the initial contact of the hand onward.

Sticking hands also opens another skill set micro moment and that is qinna.

I heard a great story about a little Uechi Ryu history from Laird Elliot, about how Uechi Ryu started using Sticking Hands. I had always assumed being from Southern China it had been part of the system.

But no, it was incorporated by Jim Maloney (10th Dan Uechi Ryu see acknowledgements and about the author.)

When Bruce Lee came by the George Mattson's dojo (Mattson Sensei brought Uechi Ryu to North America) way back when to do media and photos and such he also shared some training drills. One drill he shared was Sticking Hands. One of the people he shared it with was Jim Maloney.

Jim saw the value in it and made it part of his practice and teaching. And that is the lineage by which the skill set of sticking came down to me. Jim Maloney was Neil Dunnigan's first Uechi teacher and Neil was mine.

*Jim Maloney and Bruce Lee*

## Skill Set: Qinna

In our school, qinna is the art of seizing, locking, breaking, choking, and taking the Aggressor down. This is from a number of sources (in particular the books and videos of: John Painter and Tim Cartmell, etc.) including my previous studies.

When you focus on training this skill set you find the underlying principles that make them work and the relationship you have to be in to the Aggressor to execute the action.

However, once again when someone is trying to take your head off these are just not easy to pluck out of the air. I once was in a large group doing a seminar with Joe Lewis who said when he would ask grapplers how they would throw or lock him they would respond that when he threw a punch they would grab his arm. He replied "Guys there are professional fighters that never saw my hand when I hit. The only time you will be grabbing my hand is when I am helping you up."

There is a lot of truth in his comments.

However, once again, in the midst of the chaos you find that for a micro moment you are positioned perfectly to execute a lock or takedown. I call these GIFTS. You never attempt to take a gift before it is offered, but it is rude to turn one down when it has been offered. If you have trained this skill set then you will react to that moment and execute the movement. But if you have not then the moment will come and go and you probably will not know you have even missed it. The knife defence system sets you in place to accept the gifts offered.

## Skill Set: Tactical Flow

The latest skill set we have isolated for progressive drills and focus is harder to "label." It is a dragon use of the torso to absorb a push or strike with one quadrant of your torso while aggressively advancing with the other.

The purpose of the skill set is to not engage the strength of the Aggressor, but at the same time use the avoidance as a whipping energizer for a strike as you close. The progressive drills lead to some very fun stuff and a great experience. Once you crank things up within the drills the circles and spirals being generated become smaller and quicker. When you take it to more combat orientated drills you find that while you are performing this skill set there are times when movement gives you opportunity and allows you to start to see where openings will occur. This is again where the skill set becomes one of many and used only in that micro moment when it is the best option.

## Skill Set: Ignore the Pain

The Ignore the Pain drill so badly misunderstood by some who watched Laird Elliot on his black belt testing is another micro moment skill set. The drill is simple. One person just has to walk from one side of the room to the other. Oh, except another person will be giving them resistance with one knuckle fists into the chest, fingers into the collar bone and even fighting sticks pressed into pressure points. The drills actually have nothing to do with an intention to go directly into and through pain. However, surprise surprise, in a real fight you may just get hurt and you may be having pain applied to you to make you comply with a defeating technique and IF you do comply then you will not survive the encounter. The skill set of being able to do what you have to do and ignore the pain is a micro moment in a fight where you have to suck it up princess (a joking saying in my dojo for all genders) and take the Aggressor out anyway.

So, while it may only be a small moment in a fight that you wished never happened you may need to train to prepare yourself for that micro moment.

## The Result

Through segregating a skill set required for a micro moment in a self-protection situation we are trying to develop it to a level where when that moment happens you have the level of skill required to pull it off. Too often the moment comes and goes and may not even have been seen. But if you have focused on knowing that moment then your chances of success have increased.

**Micro moment skill set training is one of my foundation approaches and clips of a few of the drills mentioned can be found on the Wilson Practical Defence YouTube channel.**

# Acknowledgements

The first person I must thank is my wonderful wife, Andrea without whom nothing I have ever done would have been possible.

I want to thank my daughter, BD Wilson for her exhaustive and tireless efforts to edit this book into a readable format. I gave her far more work than she should have had but she did it with her usual grace and skill.

I want to thank Rory Miller for what he has taught me, for his honest feedback that made this book so much better and for writing the foreword to this book.

I want to thank my long-time training partner and Taiji instructor Rick Bottomley. Much of what underlies the mechanics of this system is due to my working with this awesome man. His feedback on the book was dead on and exceptionally useful.

I need to thank some other training buddies. Chris Beaton took all the photos in the book and did almost all of it in one shoot – fantastic guy and photographer.

I want to thank my other training partners who not only helped perfect the system but stepped in to take part in the photo shoots: Rav Ruparain, Stan Tubinshlak and Adam Ahmed.

I want to thank David Elkins, Laird Elliot, Marcus Murray, Sue Glatt, Dmitri Stolyar and Randy King for reviewing and providing helpful comments on the book.

I want to thank Jim Maloney and Van Canna both Seniors and legends in my base system of Uechi Ryu for putting me on the correct path seeking to solve that dark violent side of life.

# About the Author

Rick Wilson began his intense interest in the martial arts when his grandfather, Wallace Wilson, began teaching him boxing as a young child. Wallace Wilson had boxed while serving in World War I. This set off a lifelong interest in self-defence.

Then later, as a young teen, he was briefly taught Judo by Master Masao Takahashi in Ottawa, Ontario, Canada. It was his first hands on experience with the self defence arts of Asia. It was an interest and a love that would carry on throughout his life. Rick learned an appreciation for the devastatingly practical applications of martial arts when for a short period he studied Jiu-Jitsu in his teens under Kyoshi John Therien in Vanier, Ontario.

He gained an understanding of the mental value of forms while training in Tae Kwon Do with Master Hong Park in Edmonton, Alberta, Canada.

All of this experience brought him to become a student of Uechi Ryu Karate Jutsu with Shihan Neil Dunnigan, then with Kyoshi David Mott and now, because of his focus on reality, he is on his own seeking the most effective material he can.

Rick's delving into the reality base of martial arts was heavily influenced by two legendary Seniors of Uechi Ryu, Van Canna and Jim Maloney (both holding 10th Dan in Uechi Ryu) as well as the writings and teaching of Rory Miller.

For Rick Wilson the close quarters combat aspect of Uechi Ryu with its Southern China influences was the style that suited him best. He could bring all his past experience and find a place for it. He continues his lifelong study of Uechi Ryu Karate and has established the International Uechi Ryu Pwangainuun Association (IUPA).

In 2010 Rick Wilson was honoured to be evaluated by Jim Maloney Sensei and promoted to Rokyudan Renshi (6th degree).

Rick also currently studies a version of the Chen Taiji Practical Method from his long time training partner, Rick Bottomley.

Rick closed his martial arts school after eighteen years to devote more time to his grandchildren and now runs the Wilson Practical Defence website (wpd-rc.com) offering instructional videos and seminars and is also a Senior Consultant for Randy King's KPC Self Defense in Edmonton, Alberta, a Krav Maga school.

Rick taught his knife defence system at the Alberta Peace Officers 2017 Annual Conference.

Next from Rick Wilson

# *From the Ground Up: Counter Assault Ground Fighting*

Getting knocked or taken to the ground is deadly situation. Knowing how to fight your way back to your feet is essential. Learn how to generate powerful strikes while on the ground, dispelling the myth it isn't possible.

Join the mailing list to be notified when the new book is released!

## http://wpd-rc.com/book-list/

As a trained martial artist would you like more depth of knowledge and understanding in your training?

As a LEO or security would you like to be more efficient and effective using your prescribed techniques?

As a citizen would you like efficient and effective self defence training?

## wpd-rc.com

Members receive access to over two-hundred instructional video clips and an interactive forum. Information on seminars and private or semi-private lesson also available.

***Our Promise: To increase your efficiency and effectiveness
in practical self defence.***

# What people say about Rick Wilson

I have known Rick Wilson for the past 16 years, our first meeting coming about at an International Uechi Karate Federation Summer camp held yearly in the Massachusetts Cape Cod area. He had previously become a regular contributor to a forum which I moderate online
http://www.uechi-ryu.com/forums/viewforum.php?f=2

Over time I came to realize that Rick Wilson had devoted decades to the study of the traditional and modern tactical concepts of martial arts and their application to personal defense and survival, by always researching, designing and incorporating new ideas and methods while associated with the very best in the field such as Rory Miller and Marc MacYoung just to name a few.

I feel that Rick's clarity of his thinking and teaching is unparalleled, his honesty is unusual, and he is an incredibly gifted teacher, much in demand.

Rick exhibits a great depth and breadth of human understanding and behavior, has an amazing amount of knowledge, talent, and experience in martial arts. His instruction is world class and his martial arts classes are a great learning experience.

But most important from my point of view, Rick has extensive experience in other tactical aspects of self-protection which helps improve understanding of strengths and limitations of techniques.

— **Van Canna, Judan (10ᵗʰ Dan), International Uechi Karate federation**

Five out of five stars!!!! I was a law enforcement control tactics instructor for 10 years (recently left) and during the course of this career path, I had the opportunity to train under Rick. Rick is humble in his approach, easy to talk to, and a ton of fun to train with! After my first training session, I was hooked and still attend classes today. Rick blows my mind every single class with his ability to teach and explain the principles behind every skill we train. Not only am I impressed with the wide spectrum of skills being taught, I am most impressed with the creative drills Rick has developed to hardwire those skills. His drills are fluid, realistic and will force you to problem solve throughout the confrontation. His understanding and articulation of self-defence strategies will provide any student with the tools necessary to effectively justify his/her actions if they were to find themselves in a physical confrontation. I highly recommend that anyone takes advantage of any opportunity where they can train and learn from Rick, your training experience will be like no other.

— **Rhonda Lent**

I would recommend Rick Wilson, he's the thinking man's Martial artist, along with being totally in the know in relationship to real world self-defence. I have learnt a great deal from Rick and continue to do so.

— **The late Max Ainley, United Kingdom**

About ten years ago, after ten years of training, I began to move on a path away from the traditional dojo karate I had done, towards work that was more real and effective. I've had huge support from Wilson Practical Defense and I find the material slots fantastically well into the other principle-based training I now do (Systema).

In fact WPD is exceptional. Rick Wilson's approach is uniquely systematic and scientific with absolutely no bullshit. Its technical, but not about technique. Just efficient and effective.

Rick's martial knowledge and experience are extraordinarily wide-ranging, particularly in the areas of body mechanics, mobility and experiential, reality-based training. He has a vivid understanding of the brutalities of violent conflict and yet is able to teach with wisdom and compassion.

This stuff will work for anyone - from the beginner looking for some self defense basics to the experienced martial artist looking to transcend the limitations of "style". I actually can't recommend Rick Wilson and WPD highly enough.

> — **Sue Glatt, New Zealand**

Although I currently study Uechi Ryu – the same base style as Rick – over the years I have trained variously in Hawaian kenpo, Chito Ryu, and Shotokan, and believe that the lessons I received from Rick would provide no less insight to practitioners of other, more linear karate styles such as these. Crucially for me, Rick's instruction did not just emphasize the "how" but also the "why", and it is the "why" aspect of his teaching that has allowed me to better understand my karate in the broader context of self-defence body mechanics and strategies. Not just my Uechi Ryu, but also the karate I retained from my earlier training becomes newly intriguing when considered in terms of the "why" of self-defence body mechanics and strategy.

I count Rick Wilson among figures like Iain Abernethy and Patrick McCarthy who are at the forefront of the revival of karate as an effective system of civilian self-defence as recorded in kata and consider myself quite fortunate to have had the opportunity to receive his instruction. I would recommend his instruction to any martial artist interested in training realistic stand-up self-defence skills and to any karate-ka wishing to deepen their understanding of the practical application of their art.

> — **Stephen Hinchey, Gokyu (Uechi Ryu), St. John's Newfoundland**